TURNOVER IS VANITY, PROFIT IS SANITY

9 1/2 STEPS TO IMPROVING YOUR PROFITS & CASHFLOW

TURNOVER IS VANITY, PROFIT IS SANITY

9 1/2 STEPS TO IMPROVING YOUR PROFITS & CASHFLOW

DAN BRADBURY

ISBN: 9781691215331
Independently published by Amazon KDP

Copyright Dan Bradbury 2020.

No part of this work may be copied or reproduced without written permission from the author.

The content contained within is based on the views and experiences of the author. The author is sharing this content to serve as a guide for others who seek it. The author is not responsible for any results of the implementation of this information.

This work was produced in collaboration with Write Business Results Ltd. For more information on Write Business Results' business book services, please visit our website:

www.writebusinessresults.com or contact us on: 020 3752 7057
or info@writebusinessresults.com

CONTENTS

Dedication		6
Acknowledgements		7
Introduction		8

PART 1: DEFEND — 13

Chapter 1:	Risk Mitigation	17
Chapter 2:	Reducing Expense Ratios	29
Chapter 3:	Retention of Existing Clients	45

PART 2: DEVELOP — 61

Chapter 4:	Repeat Purchase Rate	65
Chapter 5:	Raising Average Order Value	77
Chapter 6:	Ramping Conversion Rates	91

PART 3: DISRUPT — 103

Chapter 7:	Reaching Ideal Clients	109
Chapter 8:	Referral Systems	119
Chapter 9:	Rolling Up	135

Conclusion	151
About the Author	156

DEDICATION

To Summer, Jenson and India.

For showing me the purpose of life, and for teaching me to love, laugh, live, grow and give.

I love you.

ACKNOWLEDGEMENTS

So many people have made this book possible. To Kevin. Ever the coach. Always putting the clients first. It's an honour to serve with you.

Julie, thanks for tolerating me! And for telling me where I can go when I need it!

Keith J Cunningham. Chairman of the Board. There has been no bigger influence on my core business philosophy. I've been studying with you for over a decade now. I'm still learning! Thank you for teaching me how to think. I'm eternally grateful.

Georgia, thanks for making this book a reality. It was stuck in my head for nearly two years before you helped me to free it.

Chris M, we've been through so many storms! But wow, what a ride!

Chris H. The voice of reason! Thanks for talking common sense into me on a far too frequent basis!

INTRODUCTION

As I look across the table at Dave, he begins to cry. He's supposed to cry. He has no idea how this happened.

Dave looks like a broken shell of a man. You can see that he's ready to crumble under the pressure. He's about to be made bankrupt; he'll lose his house, and his wife has no idea. He doesn't know how to break the news to her; he can barely believe it himself.

You see, Dave is a poster child for success. To the casual observer, he has everything you'd expect a successful businessman to have: a fast-growing company with millions in revenue, 15 employees, a personal assistant, a nice BMW. The list goes on. But it was all a façade. I knew, and he was coming to realise, that success isn't about getting rich in the first place, it's about maintaining that wealth.

Turnover is vanity; profit is sanity; cashflow is king. It's a saying I'm sure you've heard before. But what does it mean, and how does it apply to Dave?

Dave thought he was doing everything right. What he didn't realise was that his focus was misplaced. He spent so many years working hard to become the picture of success that he lost sight of what success actually is. It's playing the long game; building a company that can grow sustainably and turn a profit.

When I met Dave, he thought his problems were a lack of money and a lack of customers. But those weren't the problems; they were how the real problem was manifesting itself in the business. The root cause of the problem was his

Introduction

lack of clarity about what had caused things to go wrong. He couldn't see it, and as a result he didn't have a clear strategy to get himself out of difficulty.

You don't want to be like Dave, waking up one day to realise that your business is on the verge of collapse. You're smarter than that because you understand that building a successful, profitable, sustainable company takes time. You know that the end goal is to have a company that's not dependent upon you; one that can not only function, but excel without you.

As I looked at Dave that day, I could see all of this was slowly dawning on him. He was on the brink, but he hadn't gone past the point of no return. I was there to throw him a lifeline. That lifeline is the process I'm about to share with you in this book. By following this process, Dave turned his business around.

Notice that it was Dave who turned things around, not me. He was already capable of doing what needed to be done; what he lacked was the ability to think about his business differently. With the right guidance, he had the power to change everything.

We started by identifying the weakest links in the business. This wasn't a miracle cure, and initially, progress felt slow. But by the end of the first year, Dave had gone from making a loss to making a sizeable profit. A full year later, that profit was even more substantial. Not only that, but he'd hired a Managing Director who was running the company. Dave was still actively involved in the business, but there was no need for him to handle the day-to-day running of the company. Dave is making more profit now than he was in revenue a few years ago. He even received a multimillion-pound offer for the business from a larger, overseas competitor with venture capital backing. He turned it down because he'd rather keep hold of his very profitable, growing business than have a single lump sum of cash.

The Dave who sat crying across the table from me just a few years ago is long gone. He's cleared his personal debt, moved into a beautiful luxurious house, and now his success isn't just a façade, it's the real deal.

Why have I told you about Dave? Because you need to understand that what you think is the problem often isn't the problem. I don't want you to end up like the Dave I met a few years ago.

If you're reading this book, you've already taken the first step towards a more successful future. You understand that for your company to grow, you need to grow as a business leader. You need to develop skills to allow you to work at a more strategic level. Maybe you're constantly getting sucked *into* the business and that's stopping you working *on* the business. Maybe you're finding it hard to recruit the right team. Or maybe every time you try to grow, your margins are squeezed.

This book will help you lay the foundation for profitable and sustainable growth. The 9 1/2-point checklist I'm going to explain will emphasise the underutilised assets in your business and show you how to use them to your benefit. It will also identify the choke points and show you how to free them up.

This is a checklist that I've honed over 15 years, during which time I've built, bought and sold more than a dozen companies. That's included some spectacular failures, and it's these that have taught me the most important lessons. They're lessons that I'll pass onto you in this book. I've made the mistakes so you don't have to.

But more important than my own experiences are the experiences of the hundreds of business owners I've helped. They're people just like you, who are ready to grow and who want to do so profitably and sustainably.

I believe that small businesses drive the UK economy. They're where true innovation happens, they're responsible for the majority of job creation, and they're going to change the world. But they are also the most underserved and under-rewarded part of the economy. I see the impact that problems have on small business owners every day. It can be brutal, and not just in a financial sense. These problems cause divorce and mental health issues. They stop great business owners who have fantastic products and services from making a difference.

I want to change that. I'm passionate about helping you get unstuck and I want this book to act as the switch to your lightbulb moments. Each chapter will help you realise just how much you don't know, but will also show you how you can get past any blockages and rapidly grow your company. If you're ready, we'll start turning on the lights.

PART 1

DEFEND

What I want to start with isn't sexy. It isn't glamorous. But if you want to have a successful business that scales efficiently and achieves sustainable growth, it's essential to start with a solid foundation.

The first three chapters in this part explain the three essential elements you need to put in place to build that solid foundation: risk mitigation, operational efficiency and the retention of your existing clients.

By *Defend* I mean defending what you have now. This means not getting caught up in the idea that to scale you have to change what you're doing. When people want to grow they'll often say that they're not happy with where they are now. They feel like they're too small. And because they don't like what they see they'll throw it all in the bin thinking that they can do something much better.

But this metaphorical throwing the business in the bin, and by that I mean doing things like overhauling your website or product range, doesn't go to plan. It takes longer and costs more money than you think. All of a sudden, you find yourself in a blind panic and that's when you start doing all kinds of stupid shit. Before you know it, your business is failing and you're not sure why.

Defend is also about future-proofing; understanding that it's much easier to be open-minded and facilitate growth when you're in a strong place and have that solid foundation. It's also about having the confidence in the foundations you build to support a much bigger business.

I'm going to show you how thinking first will allow for the growth that comes later to happen much more quickly. This is the stuff that most people won't do, and that's why most businesses don't succeed as they should.

They overreach. They underestimate everything. That's when the foundations crumble, and the business falls apart. We all know the saying that everything takes twice as long and costs twice as much as you think it's going to. But I recently heard a Fortune 100 CEO say that whenever they're thrashing out a project, they multiply the resources they think they'll need by pi. That means they do more than double, they times everything by 3.142. And that's really smart.

The average ambitious entrepreneurial CEO tends to think that everything will be quicker and easier than it is. Because they have that mindset, they impede their process and set themselves up to fail because they set out massively under-resourced.

Imagine setting out to cross the Sahara Desert. You think it's going to take three hours, so you take the equipment, food and water you need for a three-hour trek. But in reality, it's going to take three weeks. If you set off unprepared, you'll perish. The company will fail. No amount of positive thinking is going to get you through that crap.

Defend is about having the right equipment, resources and plan to get you across the desert. You need to have a realistic view of how long something will take and how much it will cost, as well as confidence in your ability to scale successfully.

Within your business, it's about taking the time to build these deep, strong and well-placed foundations. You're not building a bungalow; you're building a skyscraper. Let's look at each of the essential components of your foundation, starting with risk mitigation.

CHAPTER 1

RISK MITIGATION

"The less risk you perceive, the more risk there is."

– Howard Marks

This quote is true of many business owners. Often we're guilty of thinking that the grass is greener and assuming that the future can only get better. But the reality is that it can get a lot worse a lot quicker than you think.

Perceiving risk doesn't mean you can't progress. It means that you've got to progress intelligently and mitigate those risks.

> *"If you could undo or rewind three big decisions you've made in the last ten years, how much more successful would you be, and how much more money would be in your bank account right now?"* – *The Road Less Stupid* by Keith J Cunningham.

I want you to answer this question.

The answer for most people is a fuck-tonne. When you look back, you'll realise that the reason you made those poor decisions was that you either underestimated risk, or you flat out didn't see it.

When you unpick those decisions now, with the knowledge you've got, you'll see where things weren't going to work, where you should have allowed for something to happen, or put measures in place to counteract something else.

PRE-MORTEM

"I just want to know where I'm going to die so that I never, ever go there."

– Charlie Munger

A post-mortem is an investigation to find the cause of death of a person. You do it once someone is already dead (a little like that last exercise). In a pre-mortem you think of the most likely ways your business is going to die, and then plan ahead of time to prevent them. And that's what a pre-mortem for your business is all about. You want to know all the risks so you can take appropriate steps to minimise the likelihood of them happening. And if one of those things does occur, you're going to minimise the damage it can do.

An ounce of prevention is worth a pound of cure

When you're carrying out exercises like a pre-mortem on your business, it's important to know why you're doing it. If you look at the failure rates for small businesses, it's enough to put you off getting started at all. The majority fail in their first year, and many more have failed by the time they've been going for five years.

Most of those businesses will have planned for the year ahead. It's not uncommon to hear small business owners saying that they've planned this year better than the last, but still they run into trouble. Running a small business is risky, so the reason you carry out a pre-mortem is to make it safe by reducing those risks.

Why, even if you've planned, does a business have problems? In my experience, it's because business owners get distracted by firefighting, and that takes their attention away from the most important things. If you want to move forward quickly and more efficiently, you have to make the best use of your time. That means you shouldn't constantly be dragged into dealing with day-to-day problems in the business. If you're firefighting, it means you haven't done enough to eliminate risks. A crisis will arise because you didn't put the right process in place to prevent it.

An ounce of prevention is worth a pound of cure. If you mitigate risk, it's going to be a hell of a lot easier to grow your business. Not only that, but you're going to be a lot less stressed and have a lot more fun because you'll be focusing on the more important and enjoyable things rather than getting distracted by the bullshit.

It's a lot quicker to anticipate the risks and mitigate them ahead of time, than it is to be reactionary and wait for the crisis before you do anything. Think of it like this: it's quicker and easier to defuse the bomb than it is to clean up the mess and rebuild after the bomb has exploded.

DEALING WITH ENTREPRENEURIAL RISK

I define entrepreneurial risk as anything that might disrupt the future revenues and profitability of the business. That might be very broad, but you can't escape from the fact that if something is going to interfere with the sales, marketing or operations it's going to be disruptive. Either in terms of maintaining the business you already have or propelling it forward.

The challenge is that often the biggest risks are the ones you don't see. Being an entrepreneur is risky; it's a lot like trying to cross a motorway on foot. How do you get to the other side? Do you race across without looking and hope for the best, or do you look at the traffic, see when and where it's moving and what lane it's in? Even if you can see the traffic, it's risky to cross the motorway on foot. But you've got a lot more of a chance of making it across than if you race out blindly and don't see something coming.

I want to introduce you to two good habits, or processes, that will help you identify and mitigate your entrepreneurial risk.

The first is to ask yourself: What could screw this up? I like to think of this as being positively paranoid. You're not being negatively paranoid by always thinking the worst and having deep, emotional reactions to it. All you're doing is considering what can go wrong. If Murphy's Law was to be true, and everything that could go wrong did go wrong, what are the things that are going to seriously damage your business? Once you've got that list, the next step is to figure out what you can do to minimise the chances of that occurring.

This isn't negative; it's prudent. You're being a little cautious, but that's positive because you're being preventative.

The second good habit to get into is learning vicariously. No matter what sector you work in, there will be people and businesses you can learn from. Fundamentally, businesses from every industry are the same. They have a marketing team, a sales team, an HR function, a legal function and so on. There's no point in reinventing the wheel when you don't need to.

Stand on the shoulders of giants, and you'll see a lot further. You don't have to make the same mistakes they did, you can learn from them. Learning from the experiences of others is critical to your success.

People often say that the best offence is a good defence. Everyone likes to see attacking football. But nobody has won the Premier League without a solid defence. It's hard enough to score goals, but even if you can score multiple goals, you're not going to win if you concede more than you score. How do you give yourself more attacking chances? You keep the ball out of your own half by having a solid defence.

FIND YOUR SINGLE POINT OF FAILURE (SPOF)

Looking for your Single Point of Failure (SPOF) is vital. You might have more than one SPOF. You need to find them all. I'll give you two examples of how a SPOF can kill a business.

I had a great business that was almost entirely automated, made on one part-time virtual assistant and making six figures in profit. This business won me a Porsche at an international marketing competition because I'd done such a good job. I took it from a standing start to over half a million pounds in revenue in ten months. And yet, within three months of me winning that award, the business was dead. What killed that business was its SPOF.

I only had one source of customers, and that was one marketing platform. When that marketing platform went away, I had no customers. It's simple, and it was an obvious risk, but at the time I didn't see it because I was young and stupid.

The second example demonstrates what's called a density risk. This is where you've got one customer who makes up a massive chunk of your revenue. We all know people who have a business that's doing well, but it's all hanging on one big government contract or one contract with a major retailer. If that goes away, so does the business.

In my case, my density risk came in a slightly different form. I had a company that was doing a few million in revenue and had thousands of customers, but 98% of sales were processed on credit cards. I only had one merchant bank that I used to process all those credit cards for my thousands of customers. I'm sure you can see where this is going.

This SPOF was the merchant bank. They were concerned because the business was growing too quickly. They're exposed if a company that's growing quickly goes bust because they have to refund the people whose credit cards they have processed. So they froze my merchant account, and, within a few weeks, they had over £64,000 of my money. It took me 14 months to get that money back.

Even though every single one of those customers had a contract, even though most of those customers had bought from us before, even though everything was in order, even though the company was solvent and there were my guarantees on it, it didn't matter. The bank didn't care. And even though I think they were being entirely unreasonable, it was still my fault because it was a single point of failure that I hadn't identified.

Now I always have at least two merchant banks for each business that I've got. These disputes do still happen when you've got fast-growing businesses, but it's incredible how much more quickly they get resolved when you say, 'Yeah, okay, don't worry about it, I'll refund the customer using your merchant and then process it using my other merchant.' Very quickly the merchant bank gets over its problems and lets you process the payment.

RISKS IN A CHANGING LANDSCAPE

There's no denying that the rate of change within the world of business is much faster than it was and, as a result, there are many more risks. But the speed with which things change isn't an excuse to be reckless. If anything it should make you more prudent as a business owner.

Many businesses don't see their approach to changing technology as reckless. Instead, they're scared of being left behind if, for example, they don't adopt this fancy new software platform. But what about when that software platform isn't as good as they thought it would be, but all their marketing has been transferred because they didn't want to miss out? It was their fear of missing out that pushed them to make the transition too quickly. They should have been more cautious, and waited a little while to see if it really did change everything.

There will always be a shiny, new platform that's going to be the sexiest thing in the world. But not many deliver. I think that the only constant is change, and that brings you back to Warren Buffett 101 and his two rules of investing: Number One, don't lose money. Number Two, refer to rule number one. His attitude to investing is that compound growth can make you very, very rich and I think that's also true in a business sense.

In a business, if you just apply the fundamentals, making progress over time, then your business can compound to a massive size. However, if you go for an aggressive approach and adopt the attitude that you need to win overnight, you might occasionally win big, but a big win is often almost immediately followed by multiple, massive losses that leave you further back than where you would have been if you'd taken a more systematic approach.

I'm not saying you shouldn't take risks, because all entrepreneurs have to take some risks; otherwise, there's no gain. But you have to manage those risks, and avoid the temptation to be reckless or just fucking stupid.

I'd like to tell you a story about a close friend of mine who we'll call Steve. In our early 20s, Steve and I both started out completely broke. Steve established quite a successful business, working for himself, where he was earning a good six-figure income, around £200,000, for most of that decade.

Meanwhile, I'd made millions, and I'd lost millions. I'd built big things; I'd had companies fail and plenty more in between. On the cusp of my 30th birthday, I made my first big exit and sold my company for £1.05 million and I thought, 'Oh wow, I've made it'.

The irony was that Steve, who was also just turning 30, had a lot more money than I did. And he'd done it much more easily, with much less drama. While I'd had a decade of ups and downs, Steve had just been steadily banking away, making his £200,000 but only living off £50,000-£60,000 and putting the rest into safe long-term investments and properties. Of course, they all grew in value and therefore so did his net worth, making him completely financially free in many respects.

I compared his journey to mine. Yes, I'd just had a huge win with my big exit, but I'd been lucky. I'm infinitely more successful than a lot of entrepreneurs who went down the same path, but that was probably a lot more to do with luck than by achievement.

Steve personifies the underlying ethos of risk mitigation. He had less stress, had much more of a life, and still came out with a successful business. I've learned that business is a lot more fun if you cut out the woes. Of course, you're going to get some of the highs, like when you win that big contract, but you can also cut out some of the bullshit and some of the risk.

When you're ambitious, it can be easy to have eyes bigger than your stomach. You take on too much, and then inevitably you overlook something and fuck it up because you tried to cross the motorway without looking first.

THE JOHARI WINDOW

The Johari Window[1] is a cognitive psychology tool that's designed to help you better understand your relationship with others. There are four elements to it, but from a business and

---

1 https://en.wikipedia.org/wiki/Johari_window

risk management perspective, there are two that are particularly important: your blind spot and your mask.

Your blind spot is the risk you're not aware of. Remember that the less risk you can see, the more risk there is. As an example, if I categorically don't believe that there's any chance of me dying in a car accident, I'm more likely to drive without wearing my seatbelt.

And yet, as soon as I drive without my seatbelt on, the chances of me dying in the event of an accident have just gone up. You can see it at those road junctions where there aren't any signals, or rights of way that are clearly enforced by road markings or signs. But statistics show there's less likely to be an accident at a junction without signs than one with signs. Why? Because people get lazy. They trust the road, so they don't see that someone else isn't trusting the road, and then they crash into them.

Your mask is really your ego. It's when you think you know what you're doing, or you come across as though you know what you're doing, but really you don't, and you're afraid of how you might look if you say, 'My business isn't together, there's risk here. There's a chance we could get this contract wrong, or we could be under-insured, or we don't have enough support if this person leaves the team' and so on.

You stick your head in the sand; you tell yourself it'll be ok if someone leaves, or if you need to claim on the insurance. But then the problem hits and the whole business gets fucked up. The root cause of that problem was your ego. The symptom might have been that you were under-insured, but the real reason things went wrong was that your ego got in the way, and you weren't prepared to admit that you were vulnerable and take the appropriate preventative measures.

QUESTIONS TO ASK YOURSELF

Every business will benefit from looking for blind spots, or for areas where our ego has got in the way. With that in mind, I want you to ask yourself the following questions:

- What are the biggest single points of failure in my business?

- If, one year from now, this business has failed, what are the five most likely things to have caused its failure; and what can I do to either minimise the chances of them occurring or minimise the damage caused if they do occur?

Apply this to my example about the company that got into trouble because of the merchant bank. Could you run your business in a less risky way, which makes it less likely that your merchant bank will freeze your account? That might minimise the risk of it occurring, but to minimise the damage, you also need to have a second merchant bank.

You have to think around every risk you uncover and find ways to reduce it or eliminate it. Think of your business as a building. Each time you minimise a risk, or the damage something could cause, you're making that building more robust. It can withstand any storm, has flood defences, is earthquake-proof, bomb proof and so on.

As a business, that means you're ready for the tough times, and when your competitors start faltering, you'll get their customers. If you look at companies that dominate in any industry, you'll see that they've normally taken the lead when the industry goes through tough times, because they're more robust, stronger, flexible and adaptable. They thrive because they're better able to adapt to the challenges that the whole market faced. They'll increase their market share and then prosper when the competition has fallen by the wayside.

I'll leave you with one final thought in this chapter:

When asked for the 'secret' to his success and immense personal fortune, Warren Buffet reportedly replied with his now infamous two rules of investing;

> *"Rule No. 1: Never lose money.*
> *Rule No. 2: Never forget rule No. 1."*

CHAPTER 2

REDUCING EXPENSE RATIOS

The first thing you have to understand in relation to operational efficiency is that bigger doesn't necessarily mean better or more profitable. If you don't have the right processes in place, if you don't have that strong foundation, all you're doing as you're getting bigger is magnifying the inefficiencies.

When I talk about operational efficiency, I mean return on investment (ROI). Every pound your company spends is an investment. It's an investment that will either bring you new customers or help you keep the customers you've already got. There might be a couple of exceptions, but broadly speaking, any money that your company spends will, either directly or indirectly, go towards those two things. This concept is from *The Road Less Stupid* by Keith J Cunningham.

That's not to say that every investment a company makes is a wise one. In essence, operational efficiency is making sure that you're getting the maximum return on your investment.

As a business owner, some of the things you spend your money on will bring you an amazing return. Some will deliver a poor return, and others might give you no return at all. When I'm making an investment in a business, it doesn't matter what that money is for; I expect it to give me a return.

The problem is that most business owners are overly optimistic about what they'll get back from an investment, and they massively underestimate the risk. It's what we talked about in Chapter 1, where things take twice as long, cost twice as much and only work half as well as you thought. That means a lot of money is wasted.

In Chapter 1 we talked about how not to kill your business. That should always be the first part of your foundation. Once you've made sure you're not going to kill your business, your next step is to make it healthier. We want it to improve, and that's where operational efficiency, and more specifically reducing expense ratios, comes in as the second part of your foundation.

There's a theme here though. This isn't sexy. In fact, it's entirely unsexy. But the fact that it's unsexy means that most people won't learn how to improve their operational efficiency. On the plus side, that means if you're one of the people who is willing to tackle these unsexy foundations of business, you'll have a significant competitive advantage.

This step is about finding the best bang for your buck when you're investing in your business, as well as going through your expenses and cutting unnecessary costs.

SPEND MONEY TO MAKE MONEY

I want to be perfectly clear; I'm not saying don't spend money. I believe you need to invest in any business you're trying to grow. The adage 'spend money to make money' is still true. However, you have to invest money in the right things and make sure you're not wasting money by investing in poor quality things.

Where this approach falls down is when people use this as an excuse to spend money now because they'll make more later. It becomes a justification for overspending and gross mismanagement of cash.

In this chapter we're going to run through some practical steps you can take that will have an immediate positive effect on your company's finances. I have yet to come across a small business where I couldn't save at least 10% of their expenditures just by practising the steps I'm about to share with you.

Let's look at how that might translate into a real business' bottom line You've got a business that's generating £500,000 in revenue and giving you £50,000 in profit. That means £450,000 is being spent; on salaries, marketing, office costs, investments for the future; all necessary things, but either way it's being spent.

But if I'm right, I could save that business 10% of its expenditure. That equates to £45,000. In other words, what I'm going to tell you in this chapter would reduce those expenditures by £4,000 a month, or £48,000 a year, which in effect doubles your profits.

FREE MONEY

The best step in this process is accessing the free money that's being wasted in your company by reducing unnecessary expenses. That might mean cancelling subscriptions you no longer use; swapping insurance providers and shopping around to get multiple quotes; or reducing the number of users on your CRM system.

Doing all of these small, unsexy jobs will save you money, and the best part about it is that there's no risk, but the likelihood of it bringing a return on investment is virtually guaranteed. In effect, it's free money.

But most people don't bother to do those small jobs because they're small, and they're not sexy. They're looking for a big, sexy, utopian idea that's going to bring in billions, when in fact they've got money lying around all over the place. It's hidden in every corner of your business. It's £50 here, £100 there, or £500 there.

Sometimes it might be something a bit bigger. For example, you might decide you need to let one person on a team go. For many businesses that can feel awkward and difficult, but once you let them go you're saving their salary, let's say £24,000 a year, but that might not be the only benefit. With that person gone, you might see productivity in the remaining team increase, all because that person you let go was a drag on the culture in your business, and now your team is more productive in their absence.

Most small businesses could double or even triple their profitability by doing nothing more than making sure they regularly slim down, and are getting the maximum return on investments and the money that they're spending.

You've only got so much time, energy and capital to invest in your business, so you need to do what's going to give you the best return. Improving your expense ratios is the most reliable and safest way to make your business more profitable, and you do that by reducing unnecessary costs.

MINDFUL SPENDING

I want to introduce you to the concept of mindful spending. This means spending your money with awareness. Let me give you an example.

Let's say you want to get a new laptop, and you choose a MacBook Air. Don't get me wrong, I'm an Apple user, but most small business owners don't need a top of the range MacBook. Instead of spending £3,000 on a new MacBook, they could get everything they need from a much cheaper laptop that costs £1,000.

When you look at it from the perspective of what functionality you need, you should choose the cheaper option. The reason you're buying the MacBook is that you want something Apple. That's fine, but just think about why you're spending that extra £2,000, and understand that you'll have £2,000 less in your bank account at the end of the year because you're choosing a top of the range MacBook over an equally functional but significantly cheaper laptop from another manufacturer.

This isn't about not spending the money; it's about being aware of the money you're spending.

Think for a moment about contactless payments. They're great for the UK because they make it easier for people to spend money, which drives people to spend more, which in turn drives the economy.

But contactless payments aren't always great for small businesses. If you couldn't make contactless payments or have automated payments, the expenses in your business would drop. I'm willing to bet money on it. If you had to go to your bank, withdraw cash and hand it over every time you had to make a purchase your spending would fall. Because it is a little bit more difficult to do, it makes you more mindful of the money you're spending. Of course, within the business the essential things would still get paid; you'd still pay your staff if you had to pay them like that, but a lot of the non-essential spending would stop because you'd think that going into your bank was just a step too far.

It's the same with direct debits. If you had to make a monthly transfer to pay for your CRM software, I bet you'd start to challenge whether or not it was good value much more quickly, and that means you'd spend less money, be more efficient and have more profit.

This is a mindset shift. It's about being respectful of money. One of my mentors once said to me, 'Dan, money is like a good woman. Pay attention to her every single day, or she will leave you.' I think he was right. Most people are tremendously disrespectful of money. They're lackadaisical about it, and that means they often don't have much. In the margins of a lot of small businesses, that's the difference between them making a 25% profit margin, a 10% profit margin or no profit margin. It might only be a few grand each month, but when you've got a £500,000 business and are wasting £100 a day, all of a sudden you've slashed your profit by half.

SURVIVAL MODE AS A STRATEGY

At some point, the UK will enter another recession. When that happens, all the big companies will make cuts. The reason they do that is that they become fearful about their long-term returns on investment. They want to make the company safer and more secure, and they know the best way to do that is to cut back on the unnecessary costs or riskier investments they were making to grow the company. Doing this immediately makes the company more profitable, which returns cash to the business and makes it more stable. What they're doing is going into survival mode.

You might be thinking that you don't want to put your business into survival mode because you want to grow. But if you want to grow you need a solid foundation, because if you've got a shallow, shaky foundation, you're not going to build that skyscraper.

This is perfectly summed up by a Bill Gates quote: 'The first rule of any technology used in a business is that automation applied to an efficient operation will magnify the efficiency. The second is that automation applied to an inefficient operation will magnify the inefficiency.'

What that means is that if you're a bit sloppy with your spending and your margins are a bit tight, it's difficult to scale because it doesn't take a lot to upset the apple cart. If, however, you've got really strong margins and are tight on how you control your money, then you've got a much greater margin for error, which allows you to grow much more quickly.

When it comes to survival mode, big businesses use this as a long-term strategy to defend the company and support future growth. It's not about a company getting into trouble and scrabbling around to stay afloat; it's about keeping those foundations strong to allow you to ride out any storms along the way.

But the problem is that this is contrary to how many small businesses are run, and that's why I think so many fail. Small business owners say they want to grow their revenue and profit, but they fail to do so because they're not efficient. They haven't thought about risk mitigation.

Richard Branson is a famous British entrepreneur. You probably think of him as a big risk taker. But if you read his books, you realise that he is a pro at mitigating risks. Of course, he's taken risks because all entrepreneurs have to take risks, but he plans to minimise his potential losses wherever possible.

A great example is when he set up Virgin Atlantic Airways. Was there a risk? Absolutely. But when he bought that first plane, he actually didn't buy it. He arranged a one-year lease with Boeing so that if things weren't going well after the first year, he could give it back. In other words, he figured out how to mitigate that risk, so that if he's wrong, as he has been in the past, he doesn't lose as much. That, in turn, allows him to take more risks because the ones that do go wrong don't hurt him as much. That means he can see which ones are doing well and double down, do things like buy more planes and grow a successful airline.

WHY ARE WE OVERSPENDING?

Society has never been more optimised towards getting people to spend money. Businesses are spending billions of dollars to maximise your desire to spend money, and it's never been easier. You've got contactless credit cards, one-click ordering, plus you're bombarded by targeted advertising across a host of platforms every day. I support this if it drives the economy. However, because it's so easy to spend, it causes people to be less conscious. They spend money they haven't got, or buy things they don't actually want or that aren't really valuable to them. In a business sense, it lowers their return on their investment.

If you're spending money like this in a business, you're going to be putting more in and getting less out. You'll still be spending the same amount of time on your business, but rather than making £200,000 in profit a year, you're only making £50,000. You've slashed the return linked to the investment of your time in the business by 75%. Why? Because you got a bit sloppy.

When a company figures out how to grow, what often makes it unsustainable in the long term is precisely this: the inefficiency. They see that they're growing though, and they think, 'Great. Time to invest, let's hire more staff.' And then they end up spending even more money. Let's return to that Bill Gates quote – they magnify the inefficiency. The sales and money are coming in, but more money is also going out. It's the classic definition of over-trading.

They grow too quickly. Growing quickly isn't a problem if you've got the funds to support it, and it's done efficiently. If each additional sale makes you more money than the previous one, because your profit margins are improving, then you're good. But the average business owner has the belief that this will happen, when in fact the exact opposite happens. Because more money is coming in, they think they need to spend more. But without the efficiency to support it, this only makes their ratios less efficient.

In a lot of cases, you do need to spend to grow. But let's think about how much you need to spend.

If your company grows to ten times its current size, you're going to need to increase salaries and hire more people. But if you've got ten times more customers, do you need ten times more staff? That's highly unlikely. And when you apply that to every part of the business, it doesn't work. You take on a lot more staff, you start justifying buying a lot more equipment. Everyone gets a MacBook and a company car.

As the owner, you start to take more money out, so then senior management wants a bit more too. Then it becomes a clusterfuck. Why? Because there was more money but no awareness of spending; no delving into the detail of expense ratios to make sure you're not wasting money left, right and centre.

EXPENSE RATIO

The expense ratio is the relationship between expenditure in a company and the return that expenditure brings. You need to think of this money being spent as money being invested, and that money is expected to deliver a result. If you hire a member of staff for £2,000, you expect them to produce a certain level of output. But if they do only half as good a job, and so you need two members of staff to hit that output, all of a sudden you're less efficient. What you have to do is find a way of managing those two people, of leading them to make sure they're producing twice the output.

That's all there is to it. There's always a correlation, even though it might not be an obvious link between directly generating revenue. For instance, a customer service person won't directly bring in revenue, but indirectly they do by making sure customers receive excellent service and come back, or recommend you. An administrator might not directly bring in revenue, but they will free up some of the owner's time to allow them to find more clients.

Here's an example of a ratio that I watch. I own multiple gyms, and I know that, because of the nature of these gyms, if more than 40% of my revenue is being spent on salaries then that gym is inefficient.

Ironically, my experience is that if it goes much lower than 40%, then the customer experience suffers. But I also know that if I go much above that 40%, then I'm cutting into my profits. If I go much above 50%, I'm getting close to break even. The reason you spend on salaries is to either get new customers or keep existing ones. But you have to maintain your ratios.

Let's say I've got £100,000 a month in revenue and I'm spending £40,000 a month on salaries. That would mean 40% of my revenue is going on payroll.

Who am I paying with that money? Why am I making that investment? Because I'm paying salespeople to bring in new gym members, as well as paying the people on the front desk and the trainers to deliver classes and personal training. They all fulfil that revenue.

What you could say is that for every £1 I'm spending on payroll, I'm getting £2.50 back in revenue.

But what happens if I bring in a new trainer who is costing me £2,000 a month? To maintain that ratio, I need them to directly or indirectly be producing an additional £5,000 a month. If they don't do that, my ratio gets worse, and that means I'm less efficient with my staffing, and have become less effective at turning my payroll investment into real revenue coming into the business.

THE RELATIONSHIP BETWEEN REVENUE AND PROFIT

Have you ever had a year in your business where your revenue has gone up, but your profit has gone down? When I ask that question to an audience, the majority of people who have been in business for more than five years will raise their hands.

My next question is, have you had a year where your revenue's gone down, but your profit's gone up? The majority of people can raise their hands for that too.

My point is that revenue and profit are nowhere near as closely correlated as you think. If most people who have been in business for five years have experienced both those scenarios, there has to be another driver. That driver is how money is spent and controlled.

People often say to me, 'I want to double my business'. That sounds great, but I've done that, and it doesn't always improve things. I had a year where one of my companies went from generating £1.6 million in revenue to generating £2.85 million in revenue.

When I was making revenue of £1.6 million, I was making £400,000 in profit, a net margin of around 25%. That's a great margin.

When I had revenue of £2.85 million, I made £250,000 in profit. That means that the £125,000 extra each month I was making in revenue cost me personally, as the sole shareholder, £12,000 a month. As my Dad told me at the time, 'Son, that takes a special kind of stupid.'

I can tell you the reason that happened. It was a digital marketing agency, and I got obsessed with growing the business, so I took on too many staff. What I wanted was to systemise it and make it independent of me. But I got less effective at converting payroll into revenue, and that hurt my ratio. Surely the whole point of increasing spending on payroll is to make more, not less money.

There is the argument that taking on more staff was designed to make the business less dependent on me, giving me back some time. But you try going from 12 to 25 members of staff in a year and tell me whether the business is more or less dependent on you.

The problem with growing a team is that you need someone to recruit them, someone to manage them, someone to coordinate everything. And yes, you can get people in management positions to do that for you but that all takes time.

During that transitioning phase, you'll be doing more. There's more pressure on you, and if payroll jumps from £20,000 a month to £40,000 a month, there's a lot more stress. There will be more staff problems; you'll go from knowing all five of your staff personally to not really knowing anyone or what's going on in their lives.

I'm not saying don't spend money, but when you do, be mindful about it and make sure you're doing it efficiently.

HOW TO START REDUCING YOUR EXPENSE RATIO

I'm going to give you two exercises you can do right now that will help you understand your expense ratio and how you can improve it.

Go over your bank statements

This might seem overly simplistic, but it will start to get you thinking mindfully about your spending. Get your bank statements for the last 90 days and go over every single debit from your bank in that period.

Are you subscribing to Google Drive and Dropbox, and do you need both? If you can't tell me what a transaction was for, how do you know it wasn't fraud? These are the questions you need to be asking. Comb through every line and cut out unnecessary expenses. Like I said before, it's not sexy.

If you don't know what every single debit is for, you're wasting money. I can tell you that now. I'm not claiming to be perfect, but I'm pretty fucking close.

Be proactive with a budget

Rather than sitting and waiting to see if you've made a profit, create a budget. A budget is where you estimate that you're going to spend money on X, Y and Z, and it's going to produce A, B and C in return.

Start by thinking about what you want your revenue to be. Then look at the following categories:

- **Category A:** Work out how much you need to spend to acquire that many customers to produce that revenue. That's marketing, advertising and sales spend.

- **Category B:** Work out how much money you need to spend to service those customers. That's what you need to spend on delivery costs, whether that's running seminars, gym classes etc. It's the cost of the goods sold.

- **Category C:** Work out what costs you're going to incur just by being in business. This is things like rent, paying an accountant to do your VAT return, and so on.

If you want to grow your business by 50%, you can start seeing how your expenses are going to stack up. If you grow your customer base and need to take on new staff, does that mean you'll need a bigger office, for example?

This isn't so much about the numbers; it's more about training yourself in the skills of understanding investment versus return. It's about seeing when things make sense, and understanding that you might not see an immediate return on an investment, but that doesn't mean it's not worth doing.

This process of creating a budget involves logically thinking through and connecting the dots for spending and return on investment. If you can't make a business work on paper, what are the chances of it working in reality? The answer is slim to fucking none, probably much closer to the none.

The problem is that most businesses don't think things through. If they did, they'd see that it doesn't make sense and isn't going to work. The planets aren't going to magically align and put money in your pocket. And if they do, it's certainly not going to be sustainable. If it doesn't work on paper, you save all that time and don't get to the end of the year and go, 'Well that was shit'.

Budgeting also forces you to be more disciplined in how you think about it, and therefore you're much more likely to respect your money. You're more likely to save that £50,000 of unnecessary spend and double your profits.

A LACK OF CLARITY BREEDS FEAR

I believe that a lack of clarity breeds fear and I think that scared money does stupid things. People make all kinds of reactionary decisions out of fear, and that's counterproductive. In the context of making intelligent business decisions, I believe emotion is the enemy.

The antidote to that fear is clarity. How do you get that clarity? By educating yourself and honing your business skills.

For example, I think most business owners don't have the financial literacy to understand accounting. As a result, even if they had the right data, they wouldn't be able to read the accounts and interpret what to do. Because they don't have the right education, they can't interact with an accountant or bookkeeper to access the relevant data, so they get stuck in a perpetual cycle of, 'I don't understand it so I can't make a decision, so, therefore, I won't make a decision and I'll stay reactionary.'

If we look at this from a cause and effect point of view, the only thing to do is to become a better business owner. But being a better business owner is the effect. The cause is educating yourself and applying that to your business.

It's like the guy who says he wants to have six-pack abs. You can fucking want that all day long, but until you fix the cause, the effect isn't going to change. So until you're willing to eat and exercise appropriately, you will not progress towards your six-pack abs.

And I believe that most business owners want to have a better business, but to get a better business, they need to become a better business owner themselves: cause and effect.

CHAPTER 3

RETENTION OF EXISTING CLIENTS

"How big would your business be if you'd kept every customer that ever tried you?"
– *The Road Less Stupid* by Keith J Cunningham

Put very simply, retention is not pissing off clients. It sounds simple but for most businesses is anything but. Many small businesses fall into the trap of becoming obsessed with finding the next customer, and the next customer, and the next customer. They forget about the last customer.

You have to remember that it's infinitely more profitable to retain the customers than it is to to get new ones. Look at the quote at the top of the page. For most businesses, that figure would be astronomical. If that's the case, you've then got to think, 'Why are they leaving?'

As with the previous two chapters, what I'm talking about isn't the sexy side of business. But because it's not as appealing, it's something that most business owners won't do. This is where there's a competitive advantage because you know something or can do something that others don't or won't.

The older I've grown, the more I've realised that there's only so much resource in a small business. Typically there's an inordinately large focus on acquiring new customers when if you just kept the customers you had you'd be much more profitable.

That makes total sense because the cost of delivering the service is consistent, whether you're doing it for customer A, customer B or customer C. The difference in profit margin between them comes from the marketing spend to acquire that customer. For every customer who stays with you, you're increasing your profit margin on their acquisition.

RETENTION VS REPEAT BUSINESS

Retention and repeat business are very similar, but they're not the same. Repeat business is getting people to make an additional purchase. Retention is not doing the things that will cause them to walk away from your business.

Retention is about not losing, whereas repeat is about proactively pushing for new sales. Repeat business requires you to be proactive, and that's something most business owners are comfortable with. Retention, on the other hand, relates to your ego. That's why most business owners miss it because they mistakenly believe that their business is delivering to a high standard of customer satisfaction.

HAVE YOU EVER MYSTERY SHOPPED YOUR OWN BUSINESS?

For most people, the answer is no. Often small business owners believe that they're too small and that they can't do it because the staff all know them. But you could ask a friend to mystery shop on your behalf.

I want to tell you about a company in the US that trains telephone salespeople. They generate about $10 million in revenue annually, and they only have one marketing strategy: they call companies that sell over the telephone and pretend to be a hot prospect. They record the call and transcribe it. In many cases, it's a train wreck, and they're handled really poorly. They send the recording and the transcript to the CEO of the company with a cover note saying, 'Do you think we should talk?'

That goes to show that even with someone who is a hot prospect, the staff on the end of the phone can still get it completely wrong. They provide the wrong prices, they're rude, or they just don't care.

In most cases, the reason this happens is not because the person who founded the company didn't have a good pitch, a good product, good sales scripts or even good training for their sales staff. It's because as the company grows, the quality tends to suffer and its procedures are not executed properly.

But unfortunately, most business owners are caught up in their ego. It's the 'your own baby is always beautiful' syndrome. They're too busy being a champion for their product and business that they don't take the time to stop and ask, 'Where is this broken?' They need to look at their company with a fresh pair of eyes to see these problems.

It's something we all do. Maybe you've tidied your home before a friend or relative comes round, and when they get there, they spot something you've completely missed. You were blind to it because you just did what you thought was good, or you didn't think they'd go in that room, or whatever it might be. In business terms, this kind of thing results in an awful experience, and that causes an exodus of clients.

A corollary to this is that, if you not only avoid the things that piss them off, but also proactively give them a really magical customer experience, they tend to be more loyal and generate more ongoing revenue. They tend to become raving fans and refer more people to your business. So, now for the same marketing spend, you not only get Customer A but also, at no additional cost, you've got Customers B, C and D. They've all come to your business because of Customer A.

When Customers B, C and D come to the business, you're also more likely to retain Customer A, because they need to feel congruent with it. This all ties back into what we've talked about in Chapters 1 and 2. You've got a business that is more stable because you've mitigated risks. You've got a business that is more efficient because you're not wasting money. You've got a business that retains revenue and customers, and the customers it retains are more profitable, all because you're fixing leaks.

You're preventing business leaking away due to a big risk that was unforeseen. You're fixing the leaking of cash out of the business due to inefficient spending. You're fixing the leaking of customers out of the business. For most businesses, they'll buy again and again and again, if you don't lose them.

DEDICATION TO THE CUSTOMER JOURNEY

I'm going to share a story that I read in a book called *Never Lose a Customer Again* by Joey Coleman. This book is about how to create a good customer experience, but one story particularly resonated with me. It's the perfect example of dedication to the customer journey.

This story is about a dentist and a new customer who suddenly finds they need a dentist.

I bit into this amazing dessert, and suddenly I felt a searing pain. I'd cracked a tooth. My immediate thought was, 'Oh no, I have to go to the dentist. I hate the dentist!' I have a childhood fear of them, and I'd only moved into this new area six months ago, so I hadn't even found a dentist yet. It wasn't at the top of my to-do list. Only suddenly it was.

A good friend recommended their dentist, so grudgingly I called them up to make an appointment. Coming from someone who hates the dentist, this is high praise, but the whole experience was incredible.

It all started with the receptionist who answered the phone. She couldn't have been more helpful. She moved other clients around to fit me in as soon as possible because I was in a lot of pain. Suddenly I had an appointment in three hours. While I was on the phone and she was organising all of this for me, I started to worry about the process of turning up, waiting in line, filling in the forms you have to complete when you start at a new dental surgery.

It was as though she read my thoughts. "Right, I've got your appointment all sorted. I've just emailed you all the documents you need to fill in before you come down. There's a link in the email so you can sign them all online and you won't have to wait in a queue when you get here," the bubbly voice on the end of the phone was saying.

I arrived for my appointment. The dentist was wonderful, and the whole experience was magical. I actually left

> *the dentist feeling happy. Three hours later I received a phone call from the dentist to remind me to take painkillers because the anaesthetic would be starting to wear off. I had a follow-up text message as well.*
>
> *I couldn't believe how fantastic the whole experience was. I shared it on social media, and a lot of my friends in the area had either heard how great this dentist was, or were already patients.*

How often have you heard the average dentist described in those terms? That's an impressive word of mouth referral (pardon the pun) and all because that dentist had true dedication to every step of his customers' journey.

What this dentist did differently to everyone else is redefined what constitutes a successful sale. The sales process doesn't end when someone walks through your door or agrees to buy your product or service. It continues until every part of your service is fulfilled.

Many people make the mistake of thinking that once a customer agrees to buy, the sale has been made. But that's not true. The sale is made only once their contract is fulfilled. Even if you've got a tight refund policy, things can happen that are outside of your control.

For example, if you sell tickets to concerts, the sale isn't made when someone buys a ticket to go to a gig. It's made once they've seen that artist and had a great time. If the artist gets sick, or the concert doesn't go ahead for some reason, you're going to have to refund them, regardless of your policy.

What that means for your business is that you always need to be building those relationships and creating an excellent customer experience to make the sale, keep the sale, and then get new sales, repeat sales, referrals and have happy customers.

We all know the metaphor of the leaky bucket, where you're continually funnelling in new customers because your existing ones are leaking from the holes at the bottom. That's how many small businesses operate. They're pouring more people in at the top because the ones further down aren't being managed properly.

You need to understand the difference between customer experience and customer service.

Customer service is reactionary. It's what you need to spend money on because your customers have a problem or because they're unhappy. And it's the customers who aren't happy who will utilise most of that resource through complaints, maybe even fighting legal action depending on the kind of business you're in.

Customer experience is proactive. It's about understanding what their journey and experience of interacting with you is like. The closer you get to creating an optimal customer experience, the less you'll need to spend on traditional customer service. I'm going to give you four tools that you can use to optimise your customer experience.

1: MYSTERY SHOPPING

I asked earlier if you'd ever mystery shopped your own business. I'm willing to bet you said no. But if there's only one tool you actually use, please make it this one. It doesn't have to be you who does it but find a friend or relative who can go through your whole sales process and who will give you honest feedback. This doesn't have to cost you money, aside from the freebie you're giving your mystery shopper.

Make sure you know exactly what your sales process should look like, and share that with your mystery shopper.

When big chains use this technique, they give their mystery shoppers a list of questions to answer. So, if you run a chain of cinemas, your mystery shopper might be asked whether it was clean, whether the staff offered you popcorn when you bought your ticket, or whether they tried to upsell you from a regular to a large-sized drink. They want to know if those small things aren't happening so that they can reinforce their importance and make sure their staff ask the right questions and behave in the right way.

Mystery shopping is relatively simple, doesn't have to cost you much (if anything) and is an easy tool to implement in almost any business.

2: TOP AND TAILING

Top and tailing is a technique I learned from Steve Bennett, who's on the Sunday Times Rich List. He used to own Gems TV, a television shopping channel with over £100 million in revenue. It's a simple enough business model; people call up and order jewellery after seeing it on one of his shows.

The 'top' of top and tailing refers to having that strategic overview of the business. It's the involvement at the top of the business.

But it's the tail that's particularly interesting. It's a way of making sure that, as the business owner, you never get too far removed from your customers or your processes. For Steve, tailing meant going to his warehouse once a month and packing boxes. It meant presenting on television once a week to sell the products. It meant answering customer calls in the call centre. The reason he did all of that was that he didn't want to become so far removed from the day-to-day of his business that he couldn't identify problems. He could listen to customers and get their feedback, find out what they were experiencing and how they were feeling.

This approach is particularly relevant if you're trying to scale your business. It's quite common for business owners to want to be removed from the frontline of their company when they're scaling. They say, 'I want to work on the business, not in the business'. I completely agree, but if you take that to an extreme, it's damaging and detrimental.

That's especially the case if a business has scaled too fast. When a business owner removes themselves too quickly from a company that has scaled too quickly, they lose touch with their customers, with the connections and with the grassroots of their company. That's when the quality goes to shit because there aren't the processes in place to prevent that.

It might be that customers' tastes are changing, but your digital team isn't keeping pace; or that the customer experience becomes really terrible; or that you're throwing lots of new salespeople into the frontlines because you're growing so fast, but they aren't properly trained, so they do a bad job. Over time, that will cause your business' growth to come to a grinding halt.

Worse than that, it will move the company backwards because you've spent all that money scaling, and it ends up being lumpy. It's not a smooth, sustained path to growth. This is often what happens when companies grow too quickly and over trade.

3: SET METRICS

To improve something you have to measure it. If you know how something is performing, you'll also see areas for improvement. You only get that if you set metrics, and you gain specific ways of measuring customer retention and customer happiness.

Customer acquisition costs are rising, and they're not likely to stop. I have yet to find someone who's told me their advertising costs across all the main platforms have gone down over time. For most of them, the amount they spend to acquire new customers just keeps creeping up. The digital environment, in particular, has become more competitive. You can see that in statistics which show email click-through rates are down, for example.

All of that means it will cost more to win the customer than it used to. If that's the way it's going, then the only way to win the game is to increase the lifetime value of the customer. And the only way you can do that is if you don't lose them. This means good customer experience is a real competitive advantage.

The importance of social proof

In today's world, because of the rise and maturity of the social network, it's much easier for people to do research to help them decide whether they're going to choose to do business with you. Although this will fall into one of the later chapters when we talk about conversion rates, it's also part of retention.

Whether you're going to buy a book from Amazon, use a local service provider, or take a holiday, you're going to look at the reviews for that product or business. They might be on Amazon, Facebook, Google or TripAdvisor, it doesn't matter, because it's the volume and quality of those reviews that will help you make a decision.

This also reiterates why customer experience is so important because when people read these reviews, they want to know how they're going to feel if they buy your product or use your service. Good reviews will make a customer more confident and more likely to buy from you.

But bad reviews can be useful too. They provide great feedback on how your business is performing, and give you an opportunity to learn. I'm not saying you should turn your business on a dime because just one customer gives you a bad review, but assuming that the person who left the review is reasonable, their review represents an opportunity. Most people react emotionally, and take it personally. But if your customer didn't get the experience they wanted, and they're not being unreasonable, you need to look at why and how you can prevent that from happening again.

The reviews of your company across the different platforms are a barometer of your customer experience. You can even get software to measure reviews across different platforms. As well as looking at your reviews, consider whether there any other dirty parts that could be found with a little digging on the internet? It might just be an old news article that isn't even true, but you still need to get things like that in check. Getting your online house in order will have two positive outcomes: it will prevent your existing customers from leaving you because they have doubts, and it will encourage more customers to buy from you in the first place. The elimination of the negative, is the positive.

Switch your priorities

You need to change your priorities when it comes to your customers. Many small businesses will focus 80% of their efforts on attracting new customers, but only 20% on retaining their existing ones. But to generate new sales, you need to focus more on the customers you already have than on the new ones.

If you focus 80% of your efforts on the customers you already have and only 20% on attracting new customers, you'll probably grow more quickly than if you approach it from the other way around.

The difficulty is, people smoke from the crack pipe of rapid business growth, and they want more. They will ignore the unsexy side of building business foundations because they want more of that growth. I'm not saying businesses can't grow fast, but you don't want fast on its own. You want sustainable. There are countless examples of companies that grow rapidly and then lose all their profitability.

If I told you that you could 10x your business next year, but the following year you'd go broke, would you take it? Of course you wouldn't. You'd take 50% growth, year-on-year, becoming consistently more profitable, every single time.

Let's look at this another way. If I said, "I want to be super fit and healthy, so I'm going to work out at the gym for 24 hours straight to get there; I don't want to do an hour a day for a month," you'd think I was an idiot. Working out for 24 hours straight isn't going to make me fitter, it's just going to make me sick, injured or dead.

It's the same with business growth. There are no shortcuts. You need to put the time in consistently to see results that last. A crash diet might help you lose the weight for your wedding day, but as soon as you go back to eating normally, you'll just put it all back on. It's about forming good habits.

The only way to make a habit stick is to fall in love with it. Sure, you need to fall in love with the outcome, but you also need to fall in love with the habits that will get you the outcome!

A few years ago, I was fearsomely fit. I was strong, and I knew I could outperform most people on the streets. But whenever I looked in the mirror I wasn't happy with my body; I was getting a bit flabby. I asked some of my friends who are also fearsomely fit why, even though I did a lot of exercise, I looked the way I did. They all told me the same thing: 'Because your diet is shit.' I wouldn't have said my diet was shit, but I didn't track it or measure it. They all said I was carrying a bit of extra fat and that if I lost that, I'd get much better muscle definition.

So, I hired a coach who told me what to eat. Each week I'd check in with him, and I'd keep track of what I ate on an app. I did this for 12 weeks, and when you see the before and after pictures there's a huge difference. They're like those cliche before-and-after gym shots, it worked. It was relatively easy to do, but the key was that I did it consistently for those 12 weeks. In fact, I haven't stopped. Every day I track everything that I eat, and I've been doing that for a few years now.

People sometimes ask me if that's inconvenient, or a hassle, but I don't see it that way. It's very much a habit that only takes a few minutes. Once you get into the habit, you get that positive reinforcement of getting the results, and you get quicker at doing whatever that habit is.

It might be a habit for customer experience, sales, managing the finances, de-risking the business. It's not a big thing, just something that you do. While you're learning to enjoy the process; you're also learning to enjoy managing your business in the right way.. You'll love mitigating risk, controlling costs and making sure the customer experience is great. And when you do, the revenue growth and profit growth will take care of itself.

When you start to look at your company in this way, encompassing all the elements of *Defend*, you'll realise that you have far more opportunities for improvement internally than you might expect. Resist the temptation to constantly be looking externally for something that's bigger, better or quicker.

4: ENGAGE TO REACTIVATE

If you're reading this chapter and worrying that you haven't done some of the things I've talked about, you don't have reviews of your business to draw on for good or bad, don't worry. This presents an excellent chance to re-engage with your existing customers. By asking them to give you a review, you're asking them for their feedback. In this era of social media, people want to feel more engaged in the process. If you contact them and ask for their feedback, you're engaging them in dialogue, and you may well reactivate them as a customer.

They'll feel like they're taken care of. And their review, feedback or endorsement will support you, either directly or indirectly, in getting more customers. You'll be improving the margin on that customer acquisition, because not only will you get their repeat business, but also more new customers without the same high customer acquisition cost.

Walt Disney was a master at using customer engagement

to his advantage. He once said, 'Clean bathrooms are good marketing'. To put that in context, you have to remember that when Disneyland opened, it was competing against the grotty theme parks of the day. He didn't have a budget for a sales force, so he relied on good customer reviews to spread the word. It was all about giving them the most incredible customer experience so that they'd go away and tell their friends what a great time they'd had, how clean the bathrooms were and so on.

DEFEND WHAT YOU HAVE

That brings us to the end of Part 1. The reason why these first three chapters are the most important is that you want to defend what you have. Often we try to progress forwards, but we get blindsided and knocked radically off track; then we end up going backwards or going broke.

The second reason they are so important is they build a rock-solid foundation, which not only allows you to grow more quickly but also allows you to do it sustainably over time. Now that we've got a solid foundation, we're ready to develop this business. That can give us massive compounded returns in the bottom line, all just by finding ways to do all the things we already do a bit better.

PART 2

DEVELOP

When Dan walked into the room, I could tell he had a lot of the usual misconceptions and ideas about how a business should be run. I'd been there, made the mistakes and learned from them. I could see what was coming. I sat patiently, waiting for him to give me the usual spiel about how he had some great idea to grow his business. I almost smiled. I already knew what I was going to say...

I knew I had a successful business. I was generating around half a million in revenue and making good money. But it wasn't enough. I was desperate to break through the £1 million revenue barrier. I thought this would make me more profit. But no matter how hard I worked, how many hours I put in or how clever I got with my marketing, things stayed the same. I'd plateaued, and I knew I needed help. That's why I was here because I knew Keith would be able to help me.

He'd been in business for decades. He'd made £100 million, lost it all and then made it back again. I knew I could learn from him. Although truth be told, I also thought he could learn from me because his marketing was terrible and that's one of my strengths. Going into our meeting, I thought I was prepared. I had what I thought was a solid business plan with lots of exciting ideas to get me through the magical £1 million revenue barrier, and I was expecting him to tweak what I had, not rip it to shreds.

But that was what happened. What I thought was a plan turned out to be nothing more than a list of goals – I was about to learn that the plan is your roadmap to achieving your goals, not the end destination. But more important than that, I was about to learn the key to sustainable business growth. I finished talking, and for a moment, he just sat and looked at me. His expression was hard to read. Then he said: "Well Dan, that's probably the stupidest thing I've heard."

I looked at him, dumbfounded. I didn't understand. "How do you mean?" I asked. His response caught me off guard: "Well you did great last year, why don't you just do the same again, but do it better?" Still the penny didn't drop, "How do you mean?" Keith half-smiled at me, "You're taking on all this risk and doing all these radical new things to grow, when actually if you just develop what you've got, you'll probably find the results are significantly higher with lower risk."

And that was it. Right there was the moment when I learned the importance of nurturing a business. He was right, of course. The following year, without doing any more work, I more than doubled my revenue and tripled my profits.

What Keith taught me is what we're going to explore in this second part of the book. This is about how to find the hidden jewels in your business, the ones that are right in front of you but that you overlook because you're too busy looking at the horizon. I talked in Part 1 about how we tend to underestimate risk, but we also underestimate the upside from optimising what we already have.

My story isn't unusual among business owners. They tend to think that they need to do something new to move their business forward when they just need to become much more effective with what they've already got. The results can be dramatic too; in some cases going from not profitable or even losing money to lucrative, six-figure profits.

Develop includes three main parts, all related to maximising the value of our existing customers: encouraging repeat purchases; raising the average order value; and ramping conversion rates. You already know that I doubled my revenue and tripled my profits in a year, so let's explore the easy ways to start doing that, starting with repeat purchases.

CHAPTER 4

REPEAT PURCHASE RATE

Repeat purchases follow on from what I discussed in Chapter 3: retention. Retention has to come first because you need your customers to stick around so that they can then spend money. Repeat purchases mean actively encouraging your customers to make additional purchases. It sounds simple, but despite that, many companies fail to do this. Here's a simplified example.

> I recently bought a new shampoo by a local eco brand at a pop-up market. It made my hair feel amazing, and it smelled lovely. I really wanted more of it, but once I'd finished the bottle, I didn't know how to get more. I'd lost their details and couldn't find anywhere that stocked it.

That's a very simplistic example of a scenario that happens all the time. A customer makes a purchase and companies don't make it easy for them to repeat that purchase. If the person who sold that shampoo had asked for an email address so that they could keep in touch, they'd be able to contact all those new customers and hopefully turn them into repeat customers. In many cases, the company has the contact details of its customers but chooses not to reach out to them.

There are three main reasons why businesses shy away from contacting their customers like this:

1: THEY DON'T WANT TO BE SALESY

People don't want to come across as pushy, but the other side of it is that they believe their product is so good that it sells itself. Even if that's true, it's a very arrogant way to think, because you're not really serving your customer when you approach it in this way. What you're basically saying is that purchasing your product is more important to your customers than anything else in their lives. Don't be ridiculous. There's nothing wrong with prompting people to buy a product that they loved.

In many cases, your insecurities are also holding you back from approaching customers and just asking, 'hey, do you want more of this?'. If they like it, they'll say yes. The reason they probably didn't order any more is that they're just busy. If they didn't like it, you'll get valuable feedback and can adapt and grow. It's a win-win.

2: THEY FEEL LIKE THEIR PRODUCT HAS DONE ITS JOB

Depending on the product or service, you might think that the client doesn't need it again. But you could well be doing your clients a disservice in making that assumption. Take the example of a physiotherapist, who thinks they're incredible and can correct any back problems in one session. You go to see this physiotherapist, and when you ask when you need to come back, they say, 'You don't, you're cured.' But even if the initial problem has been fixed, that doesn't mean you're never going to need a physiotherapist again. Firstly, you're probably not going to stop doing the things that hurt your back in the first place, and secondly, it's about maintenance, keeping you in good shape to remove risk of recurrence. It's the same for your business, making sure your clients continue to enjoy the benefits of what you provide, rather than seeing them regress.

3: THEY CAN'T SEE HOW TO MAKE THEIR PRODUCT A REPEAT PURCHASE

In some circumstances, it can be difficult to see how to encourage repeat purchases. I once had a client who was a cosmetic surgeon specialising in breast augmentation. Obviously, that's a large transaction and not a procedure someone will want over and over again. But he can think of other complementary ways in which he can help his clients improve their body image.

That might mean suggesting other surgery, or perhaps recommending a personal trainer, a nutritionist, a stylist or personal shopper, all people who can help make that client look and feel better in themselves. It's about maintaining what they now have, after paying for your service. With an example like cosmetic surgery, it might mean cross-selling either directly by your business or as a referral, in which case you get an incentive for that referral.

Now we've looked at why you're not generating as many repeat purchases as you could be, let's look at what you can do about it.

MULTIPLYING MARGINS

Multiplying margins means generating additional money from the same customers. You're not having to go out there and get new customers; you're just making more off the ones you already have.

An excellent example of this comes from a financial publishing company. Their business was publishing financial news on a subscription or newsletter basis. It was a relatively low-value product in a very competitive marketplace. That meant it was very expensive to get new customers. In a typical newsletter or subscription-type business, the battle is won and lost on retention, because that's where the money gets made. In most cases, that means you'll need to keep a customer for X number of months, or maybe even years before you start making money from them.

This business was struggling, and despite trying everything, there was still downward pressure on the price. So they stopped and looked at things from a fresh angle. They figured out that they were good at getting people to buy for the first time. They had a lot of people who had signalled they were willing to spend money, simply because they'd expressed an interest in their publication about personal finance and investments. They were generating a lot of leads. These weren't people who would buy from them, because they didn't sell the financial products, but they were interested in financial products because they were reading the news and free reports.

They realised that the asset in their business wasn't the financial newsletter they were producing, but the leads and customers they were attracting who were interested in finance. So, they sold or rented that data, all those leads, through brokers to companies that could sell their financial services or products. This was all completely legal, and even though GDPR has made it harder, this is still a legitimate way to make money. When you look at this business model, the money they get from selling the leads is 100% margin, because they had already paid and acquired the data. That in effect subsidised their customer acquisition costs and made them a lot of money on top.

Joint Ventures (JVs) can be another way to go about this. These tend to be more explicit, i.e. I market another business to my customer and pass that lead on. When they convert, I get a commission. But again this is an excellent way of multiplying your margin on an existing customer. They've already used your business, so you've made money from them. By taking a commission on another sale through a JV, you're improving your margins on that customer, and making money without having to pay the acquisition costs again.

LOOK UP, DOWN AND SIDEWAYS

As with the cosmetic surgeon example, it might not be immediately apparent where to find these opportunities to multiply your margins. In that case, I'd recommend that you look up and down your supply chain, and don't forget to look sideways too.

For example, someone who's buying golf clubs is probably also looking for a golf bag. Once they've made that purchase, they're probably also eligible for golf lessons, and before they went out and bought the clubs, they were probably eligible for a golf membership.

Another way to think of it is as a timeline of purchases. When a customer comes to you, where on that timeline are they? What would they purchase before and after? What might they repeat buy? This is where you can start to look sideways, and think about any recurring services they might benefit from because of the purchases they're making.

The problem many businesses have is that they can't think beyond what they're currently offering, even though there are lots of possibilities. Take a digital marketing agency that only provides pay-per-click management services. The first step would be to make sure that they've got their clients on a monthly retainer because that's recurring revenue. But you can think beyond that.

What else can you offer your clients that might benefit them? If they're paying for pay-per-click advertising management, the chances are that they're probably also spending on Facebook or YouTube ads. You can add those things to your services. From there you could offer web design services, and instantly you've got a dozen other areas that you can explore. Copywriting for the ads, analytics of the advertising data, all of these things add value to that client.

Look at your business from a different perspective. Don't get stuck in the 'this is what we do' mindset.

REACTIVATION

You can't retain every customer. Sometimes they'll leave through no fault of your own. But they don't have to be gone forever. In fact, it's typically much easier to get someone back than it is to get somebody to buy from you for the first time. Because it's easier, there's little to no marketing cost associated with getting them back, and they'll onboard more quickly and therefore use up fewer resources than a new client.

Come back to thinking about customer acquisition margins. When you reactivate a former customer, your acquisition costs are significantly reduced, and that means they give you a much higher margin.

Any business that has been around for any length of time will have hundreds if not thousands of expired customers. There will be a percentage of that customer base who will buy again easily as soon as they're asked, because the reason they opted out was that their circumstances had changed. If someone cancels their gym membership because they got injured, it's not going to take a lot to convince them to restart that once they're fit again, for example. The underlying premise as to why they joined your gym hasn't changed – they still want to get fit, or lose weight – so if you just put a message in front of them and make it easy for them to come back, a percentage will say yes.

Sometimes you might lose touch with your old clients, but when you see an opportunity to help them, reach out. The important thing is that you go to give, not to get. Acknowledge that you've lost touch, don't fake it when you contact them, but ask if they need your help.

I've got a client who is the perfect example of this. He recently started up with me again after taking a break for a few months, all because I reached out to him. He worked with me for two years, and his business was doing well when he came to the end of his contract. I tried to persuade him to stay, but he said he wanted to take a break for a few months. We didn't entirely lose touch, and I was aware after seeing three or four of his social media posts that his business was getting into trouble. So I reached out to him, and I did it because I wanted to help him.

I sent him a message saying, 'Hey Rob! Sorry I've not been in touch. If you've got this going on, don't you think it's time we start working together again? Can I help?' He replied and said, 'You know what Dan? I think the timing is perfect; give me a call tomorrow.' And like that, I'd reactivated a client.

But the reason I love this particular story is that when we were working together, his business was making about £20,000 a month. In the three months we stopped working together he went to break even or even losing a bit of money. But as soon as we started working together again, he went back to making £20,000 a month.

I wish I could say that it was all down to me, but part of it was fortuitous timing. He took a break because he was dealing with a crisis in his business, and that's why his profits went down. But the irony is that's why I felt he needed help. You can't make people buy from you though, and just by getting in touch a few months later when he was in a different headspace, I was able to get him straight back onboard and start helping.

The lesson here is that it's important to maintain those relationships, and if the relationship has been lost, no problem, just make sure you acknowledge that and reach out with the intent of giving. While reactivation is a subsection in this book, it's an incredibly important concept that shouldn't be overlooked. So much so that I now teach it as a tenth step on the checklist in my mastermind program. So don't overlook reactivation, it's undoubtedly a great source of untapped revenue.

RECURRING REVENUE MODELS

Loyalty programmes are a great strategy for retention or repeat purchases. Fundamentally the reason any of these schemes exist, whether it's air miles or loyalty points (e.g. Nectar, Costa), is to retain customers and encourage repeat purchases.

Take air miles as an example. British Airways gives me air miles when I fly with them. If I fly with them enough, I know that sometimes I'm going to get complimentary upgrades. That's good enough for me to decide to fly with them versus going for a slightly cheaper competitor, which means they get more repeat purchases from me than they might otherwise. Of course, the more I make that choice to fly with them, the more air miles I earn, the more incentive I have next time and so on. Now I'm certain that they're not the best airline, but unless there's an extraordinary price difference, I'm always going to see if there's a BA flight going to my destination first.

If you look at any of the big tech companies, an ever-increasing percentage of their business is coming from a recurring service. Amazon has Amazon Prime; Google has Google Drive. Having a recurring revenue stream builds in the lifetime value, and having a recurring revenue will typically lead to a much higher valuation of your company because it increases the reliability, sustainability and predictability of your profits. This is why it's important to think about what ongoing service you can provide to your clients.

Subscription models, in particular, are a big thing to look at. I'm even going to say that a subscription model can work for any business and I'll give you an example of why I think that's true. Funerals are the definition of a one-time purchase, but somewhere along the line one provider came up with the idea of making this a subscription service.

Funerals are expensive, so by offering people the chance to pay monthly, upfront for their funeral costs, they've lowered the barrier to entry. It's no longer someone's loved ones going to a funeral home to make that one big payment for a funeral; it's a choice you make before you die to pay off some of the cost each month to make it easier on your family.

The customer feels secure because they sign up to a contract to pay x amount each month into a pot for their funeral costs. The funeral company will still get the same money at the end, but they've just made their underlying business healthier and more valuable because they have a more reliable, predictable and sustainable revenue stream. I think if funeral parlours can have recurring revenue models, then just about any business can. Sometimes it just takes a little bit of ingenuity.

THE VALUE OF BEING DIFFERENT

Just because other businesses in your industry don't operate on subscription models, that doesn't mean you can't. In fact, there can be a significant competitive advantage in offering something that no-one else is.

Netflix is the ultimate example of the value of being different. When Netflix launched, many people didn't understand how you could make money from a purely paid video subscription. With the internet, the rise of YouTube, and all the free channels available through Freeview, people simply couldn't see how they were going to make it work.

Netflix was the first paid subscription video service in a world where so much video content was free. And yet, they have a company valued in the billions all because in that narrow window when it launched, it was pretty pioneering and they tapped into what customers wanted that Freeview couldn't give them – complete control over what they watched when.

HOW TO START BUILDING REPEAT PURCHASES

This chapter should have given you some ideas of how to begin building repeat purchases and recurring revenue streams in your company, but don't race in all guns blazing. Remember risk mitigation from Chapter 1. Follow these steps to make sure you're defending your business first, and developing it to disrupt second.

Start by looking at the different categories I've just listed and brainstorm a variety of ideas across all of them. Then rank those ideas using the criteria:

1. How confident are you it will work?
2. What potential opportunities are there to sell this approach?
3. How can we test this safely?

That third point is critical because if you can test it safely, you can make an informed decision about whether to scale it and roll it out so that it becomes ingrained in the business, and if it does flop it won't wreck the business.

You definitely don't change your business overnight. For example, you might have a theory that by cutting your prices by half you'd win five times as many customers and still make a profit because there's enough margin in your product and overall, you'd still be better off. But you wouldn't change all your prices overnight because if you're wrong, you can't reverse the price and go back up. You risk destroying the entire business.

Testing is vital. You have to test your ideas and if they work, great, you keep them, but if they don't then you bin them without damaging the business in the process.

CHAPTER 5

RAISING AVERAGE ORDER VALUE

Let's begin by explaining what I mean by average order value (AOV) and show you why this can be a lucrative way to improve your business' bottom line. To find your AOV, you add up the value of all the invoices you've raised and divide it by the number of invoices you sent. That will show you how much an average client spends with your business. In this chapter, I'll give you some advice about how you can increase that.

Imagine we own a supermarket. If we want to grow sales at that supermarket we can either:

1. Get more people to come to our supermarket for the first time

2. Get them to spend more when they're in the supermarket

3. Get them to come back to the supermarket more frequently.

Which of those three options is the most difficult? Of course, it's getting new customers to come to our supermarket. Why? Because they don't know we exist, and they don't necessarily like us or trust us. They have a preferred provider that they want to use instead. Bearing that in mind, how much easier is it to increase the average transaction size? The answer is quite a lot because they already know we exist and are in our shop; they already have a need and the means to pay. In other words, it's infinitely easier to get more money out of someone who's already pushing a trolley around the supermarket, either by encouraging them to buy more items or to buy more expensive items.

There are several ways to achieve this, which I'll go into in more detail shortly. It's also important to understand why raising AOV comes in the Develop section. This is where we're looking at growing a company further after we've defended it from failing. Raising AOV is a sales tactic which can be incredibly lucrative, but it comes with potential risks.

We're talking about business value maximisation. How you maximise the return on your time, effort and money into your business. There are four main options to consider.

1: GOOD, BETTER, BEST

This means having premium offerings in addition to your standard offerings. You're looking at the distribution curve of your buyers and working out where to pitch each option. Airlines are a good example of where this works well.

Let's say you're booking tickets to take a transatlantic flight. On most planes there will be four ticket options: Economy, Premium Economy, Business and First Class. Why don't airlines fill the whole plane with economy seats? Because some people are willing to pay more. The airline knows it makes more per square foot in the first-class cabin than it does in the economy cabin. But if that's the case, why not fill the whole plane with first-class seats? Because there aren't enough people who are willing to pay those prices for a transatlantic flight.

It's a distribution curve. Most people are willing to pay economy; a good proportion are prepared to pay premium economy; a small chunk are prepared to pay business; and a tiny proportion are prepared to pay first class. The airlines find their balance. I would argue that it's the same for most businesses.

You need to decide what are your good, better and best options. Then the decision for the customer comes down to not whether they buy – they've already made that choice – but which option they buy. There will be some people who aren't buying from you not because you're too expensive, but because you're too cheap. By giving them a premium option at a higher price point, you're encouraging them to spend more. The margins on those higher priced products are greater and therefore you make more from the transaction.

There's another benefit to the good, better, best approach – it can increase your average conversion rates. There are a couple of ways in which this can happen, depending on the psychology of the buyer. The first is that the premium versions make the economy version seem like better value and that can remove a barrier to buying in the first place.

The second is that it can make your middle option the most appealing. Imagine you're looking at paying a consultancy for a bundle of services and they have three price points: £10,000, £12,000 and £15,000. You might look at those and think that £15,000 is too much. But with those three options, £10,000 now looks cheap, because it's one-third less than the highest priced option. So you pick the middle package of £12,000.

You shouldn't overlook the advantage of improving your average conversion rate. What you're doing with this model is increasing the number of ways people can make a purchasing decision. That means more sales, compounding your overall revenue.

2: PRICE INCREASES

Price increases are another way to increase your AOV. This also has risks attached, but if you get it right, you will see the extra money you earn from sales going straight to your bottom line. For instance, if a business has a net profit margin of 10% and it puts its prices up by 10%, it will increase that net profit margin to 20%. That means profit in that business will double, and it won't cost the business anything extra.

Depending on the business, and how much you increase prices, you may see some customers drop off, but often that doesn't matter because you still end up ahead. If you lose some customers, you also lose the cost of providing them with that service, so depending on how many you lose, you can make more money with fewer customers.

This logic is why many high street stores are happy to close for celebrity shoppers. Not only will that person spend 100 times what the average customer spends, but they also need to pay fewer members of staff to keep the store open and keep them happy. That store can afford to lose 99 customers that day because the revenue will be well ahead of the costs.

However, because there is a risk of losing customers, you need to find a way to test your price rises before you introduce them across the board. Depending on your business, there are several ways in which you can do that.

Split testing

For e-commerce websites, I'm a fan of split testing price points. That means some customers see landing page A where a jacket is priced at £100, and others see landing page B where it's priced at £50. You can see whether consumers are willing to pay that higher price for that product. If someone sees both pages, you just have to deal with it honestly. Tell them that you're thinking about increasing the price and are testing to improve the business; then offer them the jacket at the lower price.

This works well on e-commerce sites because people come and go and we're used to seeing different things at different price points, or even the same things at different price points. It's the world we live in and for high-volume e-commerce split tests can work well.

The rule of five

For smaller serviced-based businesses, where sales are closed on an individual basis, and you're not plastering your price points all over your website, I'd recommend the rule of five approach. Credit where it's due, this is something I learned from Jairek Robbins. He explained that in many cases, the issue with increasing prices isn't the marketplace, but the business owner.

They have a psychological barrier to increasing prices and justify keeping their prices the same by saying things like the marketplace is sensitive; we're already the premium offering; we increased our prices two years ago, we can't increase them again. But generally if you ask them what happened when they increased their prices, they'll tell you that their sales went up.

If that's the case, why would you not test putting them up again? And if you're worried about going too high, this is where the rule of five comes in. It refers to each batch of five customers.

Let's say your current price point for your services is £10,000. You start by getting five customers at that rate. When you get to the sixth customer, you increase that price point by an amount that's small enough you feel comfortable, but big enough that it's worth it. For this example, you go up to £11,000. You close five customers at this price point, and then you increase it incrementally again and go after five more. You keep doing this until you see that the higher price is negatively affecting responses. That might happen because the marketplace isn't comfortable with it or because the business owner loses confidence.

Either way, you've increased your prices successfully. Five customers is an arbitrary number; you can change that depending on the nature of your business. But what this approach means is that over time you incrementally inch prices up. There are several advantages to this. Firstly, it means you as the business owner have psychologically become comfortable with the idea of charging higher prices. It will also help you adapt so that you're pitching your service appropriately. You're not suddenly jumping from £10,000 to £15,000, but ultimately you could end up charging at the top end of that. The market will also adapt to your higher prices, and you're reducing the risk of seeing sales plummet overnight because you've increased your prices too much too quickly.

You can also use the incremental price increases to incentivise people to buy now. You have to do this carefully because people don't like to feel as though they're being played. The way I'd approach it is to tell the third or maybe the fourth person that you're planning to put your prices up from £10,000 to £11,000. But frame it like this: 'My price is currently £10,000, but I've said that only two more people can buy at this price, then it will increase to £11,000. I'm not saying this to pressure you, but I'm telling you because I imagine that in a few weeks my prices will have increased because I need to maintain pricing integrity. So go away and think about it if you need to, but I just wanted to let you know so you can make a fully informed decision because I'd hate it if you went away to think about it and came back to me in a few weeks when it had gone up to £11,000.'

There's no one-size-fits-all approach to this. I can't tell you how much you could or should put your prices up by. That will depend on how competitive the marketplace is, and how commoditised your product or service is. You always need to think about the big picture and make sure any price rises are appropriate.

That's why testing price increases is so important, however you do it. The most crucial thing to ask is, 'Is it possible to test prices in a way that we can overturn that decision if it turns out to be a bad one?'

Think about whether you can test it with a certain segment of your database, in specific locations if you have a multi-location business, or on particular product lines. Most importantly, can you test it for a limited period?

You also need to work out whether losing customers will mean you're losing money. So if you decide to increase your prices by X amount, think about what would happen to the percentage of people who buy, assuming you still get the same level of leads coming in. Work out your new gross profit margin, and then calculate how many customers you could afford to lose and still be ahead of where your business is now. So, if you lose 10% of your customers as a result of a price increase, will you still be making as much or more than you do now? What about if you lost 20% of your customers, or even more? At what point would you start going backwards?

Once you put your prices up, you need to track everything and see whether your assumptions about the number of customers you'd lose are correct. The damage comes if you increase your prices and are unable to undo that price rise.

Imagine that you increased prices and thought that you'd lose 10% of your customers as a result, but knew you'd still be ahead by 40% in gross profit terms. But, in fact, you lose 50% of your customers and all of a sudden you're in deep shit. The problem is, by going backwards and dropping your prices, it depositions you in the marketplace.

Another risk with increasing prices is that, if you're in a highly competitive marketplace, your customers may go elsewhere. This can be especially damaging if you raise your prices on a front-end offer, but most of your money is made on the back-end. If they don't come to you in the first place and keep buying from you, you're losing out substantially.

UNDERSTANDING SECOND-ORDER CONSEQUENCES

An important part of seeing the big picture is understanding second-order consequences. First-order consequences are what happens immediately to sales when you put the price up. Second-order consequences are what happens further down the line.

A great example of this is Black Friday sales. For some businesses, these sales can make absolute sense, but for others, it just hurts the business. Let's say you can spike your revenue by giving 80% or 50% off in the short term, but what's the downstream consequence of doing that? The second-order consequence in this example might be that even fewer people will be prepared to buy your product at the regular retail price.

Look at a business like DFS. Has anyone ever bought a full-priced sofa from DFS? Of course not because they always have a sale on. Yes, there are laws about sales and always selling something at a marked down price, but the point is that DFS has got itself trapped in a cycle of always selling products at a discount, which massively eats into their margin. That's not to say you can't operate like that, but do you want that to be how your company operates?

Apple is a brilliant counterexample. How often do you see discounts on Apple products? The answer is almost never. As

I said earlier in this chapter, if increasing your prices by 10% can double your profit margin, then decreasing them by 10% can annihilate it.

3: INCREASING PRICES ISN'T FOR EVERYONE

For some businesses increasing prices can be an easy win, especially if your company isn't in a very competitive marketplace and has a strong USP (unique selling point). But if your USP is that you're the cheapest in the market, raising prices may not be an option, or is one that carries a lot of risks. That's when focusing on operational efficiency is better.

John D Rockefeller is a brilliant example of this. He's the richest man in the world in today's adjusted terms. At the height of his oil empire, he could drill oil, get it out of the ground, refine it, ship it and sell it at a profit for less than it cost his direct competitors to just get it out of the ground. That's all due to the efficiency of his operations.

A current day example would be Amazon and Jeff Bezos. Interestingly, there are only two companies in the history of humankind that have had a trillion dollar valuation: Apple and Amazon. That's interesting because Apple is a premium provider whereas Amazon is a cheap provider. But Amazon has two things going for it, it's got the biggest range, and it's usually cheaper than other retailers.

Many of us check the Amazon app before committing to a purchase in a store to make sure you can't get it substantially cheaper online. That's how Amazon has been so successful.

4: BUNDLING

Bundling is another alternative to good, better, best or increasing your prices. It can mean two things: either you're offering a discount for buying more, or you're tying your offer into the outcome. An example of this would be if you're offering a meal deal. You know your customers are hungry and they're coming for lunch, so you're saying, don't just buy this sandwich, spend an extra X amount and you can also have these crisps and a drink. They're looking for lunch, and that's what you're selling them, not just helping them decide between this sandwich and that sandwich.

The advantage of offering discounts for buying more is that you're locking customers into buying from you and you know that customer is buying more sooner. But you don't just have to approach it from a buying more perspective. It could be that you're encouraging them to spend over a certain amount to get a premium offering, such as when an e-commerce site offers free shipping if you spend over £100. Maybe you have £90 of items in your basket, and for an extra £10, you could get the free shipping. The company has done the calculations and knows that free shipping costs them £2, so for the extra £10 you spend they're making a healthy £8.

Bundling can also take the form of extra gifts or loyalty points on a reward scheme. The key is to find additional bonuses that have a low or even no cost to you as the provider, but that have a high perceived value to the person making the purchase.

One risk to be aware of with upsells and cross-sales is that it can sometimes feel too transactional. If you're too pushy or there are too many upsells or cross-sales then it can create a negative response from somebody who's just bought from you. You've ruined the new relationship you've just established, in other words. The key is to carry out these upsells or cross-sales elegantly, and be respectful of the relationship.

That might mean you wait until you've had several interactions with them before you introduce any upsell opportunities. By this point you've created rapport, value is being built, as is the relationship, so it doesn't feel transactional when it's approached in the right way. Whether it's referrals, testimonials or upsells, they all become easier when the value has been created, so there's no risk and you don't cause damage. The damage doesn't come from the upsells that you do get, but from the ones that you don't, because they're annoyed at the attempts to upsell, and therefore don't come back to you in the future.

Bundling won't work for every business. If you're a luxury, premium provider, you're not going to want to market using discounts because it will deposition you. No one buys a Ferrari and brags about how cheaply they managed to get their deal. They talk about how much that car cost when it was new. As a premium price provider, you probably want to avoid bundling, because you want to stick with your message: 'We're expensive, and we're worth it.'

REMEMBER PEOPLE ARE BUYING AN OUTCOME

When you're thinking about your product or service, remember that the customer is buying the outcome, not the product itself. That means they'll be happy to pay a little more for your product or service if they have confidence that you'll deliver the desired outcome.

Think about the outcome your customers want when you're having those early sales conversations with them because that's what you need to sell. If you can think like this, then you're much more likely to find ways of offering additional value, which makes your company more attractive. Think back to the supermarket example at the beginning of this chapter. Your customer isn't just trying to feed themselves because they're hungry, they're trying to create dinner for their family or a special meal for their loved one.

If you're hitting that emotional outcome, it will be much easier to upsell them a more expensive bottle of wine, or a luxurious dessert. It's a different proposition. When it comes to raising AOV, you need to think about the outcome that somebody wants, and that won't necessarily be the cheapest option.

Let's return to our airline metaphor. If everyone just wanted to pay as little as possible to fly from London to New York, there'd be no need for business or first class. But people don't fly business class because they want the cheapest option. They want to look good, not feel pestered, or they're worried about how associates taking the same flight might perceive them if they don't fly business class; it's their ego that makes them choose that higher priced ticket.

Always bear in mind the emotional, internal, intrinsic reason that your client is buying a product or service. Thinking about that can be very helpful for raising AOV, and can also help you with what I'm going to talk about next, which is ramping conversion rates.

Before we jump into Chapter 6, I'd like to tell you a story about how increasing prices can also improve your conversion rates.

Many years ago, I had a business that sold distance learning education programmes via mail order. That meant customers were sent CDs and workbooks in the post. We got most of our leads through direct mail, who'd be sent a follow-up letter and brochures.

I was selling these courses for around £1000. But then someone suggested I double the price of my courses, so I split tested the price points. For the next 200-300 leads, I sent out some marketed at £1000 and some at £2000. Not only did my overall revenue go up, but my conversion rate also went up.

By increasing prices, I saw my conversion rate go from 3% to 4%, and the extra money I made was going straight on the bottom line. I quintupled the profit of this particular business by raising the prices. The reason we saw more sales per leads was because there was a perception that because it costs more, it must be a better product.

It's a great example of why it's sometimes worth taking the risk of increasing prices. If you test an idea like that, you don't always know how it's going to work out, and sometimes it can work out massively in your favour.

CHAPTER 6

RAMPING CONVERSION RATES

In this final chapter of the *Develop* section, I'm going to talk about ramping conversion rates, specifically about how you convert new enquiries into customers. Your conversion rate is how many enquiries subsequently become customers. For example, if you had 20 leads enquiring about your product or service, and four of them were to buy, you'd have a 20% conversion rate.

I'm going to explain how you can optimise your sales process to ramp your conversion rates. Every person who hears about your business makes a purchasing decision, and I'm going to tell you how you can make more of them into your customers.

The following three principles will work for any business, and by following each one you can significantly improve your conversion rates. This won't cost you more in lead generation

/ advertising spend, but it will significantly and positively impact your bottom line. It can be a real game-changer.

1. Persistent follow-ups
2. Carefully crafted messages
3. Finding your ideal clients

PERSISTENT FOLLOW-UPS

Persistent follow-ups are one of the areas where many small businesses fall down, and it's an area that you shouldn't overlook. Research[2] suggests that 80% of non-routine sales only go through after at least five follow-ups. That means if a customer has their first contact with you via an email enquiry or over the phone, you need to contact them at least four more times to increase the likelihood of converting them into a customer.

But the research shows that the majority of salespeople give up long before they make this fifth contact. Almost half give up after just one follow-up, and a further 22% after two follow-ups. That means the majority of businesses are trying to close a sale on that first interaction, and even those who try a second time aren't going the distance. They're disregarding leads that this research shows are likely to convert with a few more communications. You're effectively throwing four-fifths of your leads away, and if you followed up more consistently, your business would be five times larger.

---

2 https://www.marketingdonut.co.uk/sales/sales-techniques-and-negotiations/why-you-must-follow-up-leads

Following up more often is only one element of this principle. The type of communication method you choose can also have an impact on conversion rates. Remember that not all communication types were created equal, but also understand that they all have their place in your process.

There is certainly value to be gained by running an email newsletter campaign, where you send out an email each week just reminding them that you're there. That's what I'd describe as a high-value, low-cost communication. Obviously, that's not going to have the same impact as a phone call or face-to-face interaction, but depending on where someone is in their purchasing decision, it can still be a useful tool.

Although a phone call or face-to-face interaction can have more value, the challenge is getting a prospective customer to agree to a meeting, or answer the phone. The communication methods don't have to be mutually exclusive – just because you're sending them an email newsletter doesn't mean you can't also call them. There is value in both approaches, just not equal value.

Make sure you're using different media types to reach out to people. They're complementary and when used together can have a compounding effect. As well as sending emails, post on your Facebook page, share a video on YouTube or do a podcast.

Why don't businesses follow up more consistently if they're losing so many potential sales? There are many reasons, including laziness and impatience. But often small businesses can have a psychological barrier to following up on leads. They have limiting beliefs, they feel guilty, or they don't want to come across as too salesy or pushy. They have this misplaced faith that when the customer is ready to buy, they'll come back to them. But what we, as business owners, have to remember is that people are busy. You're not important to them, so why should they remember you? They need reminders that you're there and that they can contact you at any time.

Not everybody is ready to buy right now, but that doesn't mean they're not a good lead. You need to nurture them and put in the groundwork to convert them, don't just focus on the quick wins.

CAREFULLY CRAFTED MESSAGES

The next thing you need to think about is the message you're following up with. You have to tailor your message to suit different buyers. In many cases, you can sell the same product in different ways because it's able to meet different needs or desires. You've got to have the right message for the right person.

Think about the motivation for someone buying your product and tailor your messaging accordingly.

FINDING YOUR IDEAL CLIENTS

The third principle is finding your ideal clients. If you think about your business staying constant, with the only thing that improved the calibre of the leads you generated, that would change everything. This is about identifying who your ideal clients are, and dedicating more of your time to converting them, than clients who aren't in that group.

Let's say that the 20% of your leads who convert without multiple follow-ups are where you start looking for this ideal customer. And of these, let's say 20% are responsible for 80% of your profit. Mathematically, 4% of your leads are responsible for roughly 64% of your profit. Often the people in this 4% have different reasons for buying. Once you've identified them and their motivations, you can craft your messages to attract more customers of a better calibre. Don't treat all leads equally, because they're not. To optimise your process and ramp your conversion rates, you need to identify the highest quality leads and focus more of your time and efforts on them.

HOW RAMPING CONVERSION RATES WON ME A PORSCHE

Now I'm going to tell you how I used all those principles to take a new business from scratch to £500,000 in revenue in just ten months, and win a Porsche along the way. I achieved this with the techniques I've just talked about and only one part-time assistant. That's how effective ramping your conversion rates can be.

I won the Ultimate Marketer Contest, which is run by Infusionsoft each year. The campaign I ran was heavily automated, but it included everything I'm talking about in this chapter.

The business that won me this competition generated its leads through Google pay per click. People would opt in, and request a brochure or information. It worked, but initially, it was relatively low margin because the marketing costs were so high, so how did I fix that?

Firstly, I added extra steps to the lead nurturing process. It wasn't as simple as someone requesting a brochure and us sending one. I added around 25 steps over six months to persuade people to make that initial purchase. What we found was that a certain percentage of leads would still buy, even with these added steps. There was either no or minimal incremental cost to an additional follow-up step because we paid for that marketing spend upfront to acquire the lead. Therefore it was more profitable to aggregate that marketing spend, by following up more thoroughly with leads than to throw the dead leads away and spend money getting new ones.

I started adding more steps as reminders. This is where using different media types is advantageous, and actually, it's the key to adding these extra steps. People can unsubscribe from an email, so are you sending text messages, making phone calls, leaving automated voice messages, or sending direct mail? Do you have a Facebook group, a podcast or a YouTube video? You have to think about how many different types of media you're using, because maybe that person doesn't check their emails very often, but you'll find them on Facebook or Instagram every day.

The volume of communication is important too, because you might contact someone when the timing isn't right. But if you persist and follow up over time, you're more likely to catch them at that point when the timing is right for them to make a purchase. But my strategy for communicating with leads wasn't just about multiple follow-ups, it was also heavily based on tailored messaging, and this is probably what won me the competition.

When someone requested a brochure, we'd ask them why they were interested in our product. We were selling distance learning, so what we wanted to know was why they wanted this qualification. Did they want it to make money, work from home, or have more skills and be more effective in their workplace? People would answer that question and then we would tailor the follow-up messages based on their answer.

It's about selling the same product in different ways, because it can meet different needs or desires. Not everyone who wanted to take this course and get this qualification was doing it for the same reason. This marketing campaign recognised that. This is vital for improving conversion rates. You need to think about how you can adapt your marketing to suit what your customers want, and follow up accordingly. You need to think about how you can find out what they want in the first place.

The next point is that all leads aren't equal, and you shouldn't treat them as though they are. With this campaign, as well as asking people why they were interested, we'd ask how committed they were to taking this qualification in the next 90 days. They had to self-score on a scale of 0 to 10. That meant I could adapt the time, effort, energy and money I spent pursuing those leads based on how they scored themselves.

With this particular business, we did a lot of direct mail, but if someone had scored themselves 7 or lower, there was no point in sending them direct mail because it didn't yield enough extra to recover the cost. But if they scored themselves 8 or higher, it made absolute sense. By doing this, I reduced my costs for nurturing these leads. If you think about a regular sales team, does it make more sense for them to call the 8s, 9s and 10s two to three times, or to call everyone once?

Obviously, your sales team should allocate their time based on the likelihood of making a sale. If you can rank your leads, you're aligning your resources to maximise the conversion rate by putting the time and effort in where it's likely to be most successful. That's part of finding your ideal clients.

It's important to state that at no point did my lead generation improve. That stayed the same. What made the whole business suddenly very lucrative and what allowed it to grow rapidly was my ability to measure, test and improve each of the steps in the process. By doing all of those things, I built a profitable business and won a Porsche, all with minimal resources.

MAPPING YOUR SALES PROCESS

To know which steps to add where, and to work out how best to optimise your sales process, you need to know exactly what it is. That means you have to map it. Always start at the end. Write down the last thing someone does before they make a purchasing decision. It might look something like this:

5. They speak to a sales rep, and you expect the sales rep to close them over the phone.

4. They book an appointment to speak to a sales rep using automated software.

3. They're asked to book an appointment when they opt to download a guide on the website.

2. To download the guide, they have to opt-in on the website and fill ina form on the landing page.

1. To get to the landing page they see a Facebook ad because you paid for XYZ.

Now you have a map:

Facebook → Landing page → Download guide → Schedule call time → Sales rep call = Purchasing decision over the phone.

MEASURING EACH STEP

Once you've got your map, you need to think about how you can measure each step. Either, how do you measure that already, or how could you measure that? Again, you can work backwards, so:

6. Sales can be measured because we raise invoices.

5. Our sales reps record the number of calls they have.

4. We get a report from the scheduling software about how many people book calls.

3. We have a database to tell us how many people downloaded the free report.

2. We have Google Analytics to show us how many landed on the landingpage.

1. Facebook Ad Manager can tell us how many people clicked on the ad.

Now let's run through an example to see how many leads you'd need for a sale.

5. To get one customer, your sales rep has to speak to two people on the phone. That's a 50% conversion rate on that final step.

4. But only 50% of the people who book a call actually answer their phones for it. That means you need four people to book calls to get to the two sales calls you need.

3. Only 50% of the people who download the report will opt-in for a sales call. Now you need eight people.

2. Before that, only 10% of the people who arrive on your landing page download the report. Now you need 80people.

1. And finally, let's assume that only 1% of the people who see your Facebook ad click on it. Now you need 8,000 people to get that one customer.

IMPROVING EACH STEP

Once you know all of that, you can look at how to improve each step. Again, let's start at the top with a few examples.

5. How can you help your salespeople to close more than 50% of their calls? Give them more training? Change the scripting of what they say? Maybe change or extend the payment plan they can offer?

Take each of those ideas and rank them in terms of the ease of execution and the likelihood of them working, and test them. Start with the best idea first and test it. Each idea is going to either improve that step, make it worse or have no effect. Keep the ones that work; bin the ones that don't. If you test enough ideas, you're going to be able to improve that step, like a salesperson's closing ratio. Let's say that some of these ideas work, and you improve the conversion rate from 50% to 65%.

4. How can you make more people show up for the calls? Can you proactively call them if they don't call at the allotted time? Can you send out automated emails or a text message to remind them about the call? Test your best ideas, same as before, and keep the ones that work. Let's say by doing that, now 60% of people show up on the call, instead of 50%.

You get the idea. But what's really important to understand is that these incremental changes compound and that can rapidly accelerate your company's growth. Most business owners don't do this. They want one magical thing that will instantly give them 7,000 new customers, but that one magical thing doesn't exist. It's all about being meticulous at every step of your process, measuring everything and testing new ideas to find out what works. You're keeping the lead at one end of the process and someone making a purchase at the other, but you're looking at what you can do differently in the middle to move them further along that line.

DON'T RUN BEFORE YOU CAN WALK

This chapter brings us to the end of *Develop*. Before we move onto the final section – *Disrupt* – I'd like to emphasise why it's so important to work through *Defend* and *Develop* and not just skip straight to *Disrupt*. I know what comes in *Disrupt* can be very alluring, but without working on the areas I've highlighted in *Defend* and *Develop* things can come crashing down very quickly. Remember, this isn't about getting rich; it's about staying rich and creating sustainable growth.

I like to use the analogy of running a marathon. If you come to me and tell me you want to run the London Marathon, but you're morbidly obese and your leg is seriously injured because you've just been hit by a car, I'm not going to tell you to suck it up and go on your two-mile training run. That would be fucking stupid. I'm going to start by fixing your leg and stopping the bleeding. Then you've got to rehabilitate and learn to walk, at the same time eating more healthily. Once you're ready to start running, the next step is to learn to run faster, and that will take you through the 26+ miles of the marathon and beyond.

If you're not functionally able to run in the first place, pushing harder isn't going to work. It's just going to lead to more injuries and set you back further. However, lots of business owners are guilty of this. They've got an injured, obese business that's not healthy, but they're intent on trying to run before they can walk.

PART 3

DISRUPT

The final three chapters that fall under *Disrupt* are the most exciting part of this book. The strategies I'm about to share are some of the things that can create the fastest growth. But you'd be stupid to take these on without having the right foundations in place. This isn't the place to start scaling your business, so if you've skipped ahead, please go back to Parts 1 and 2 before jumping into Part 3.

Let me explain why the following chapters are different from what you've read already. *Defend* is about making sure things don't go wrong. *Develop* is about the things that you're already doing, but doing them better. *Disrupt* is doing something new, or approaching something you're already doing from a different perspective and employing a different strategy to drive revenue growth.

The strategies I'll give you here are exciting, but they're also higher risk. If you've got your foundations locked down by following the advice in *Defend* and *Develop*, these strategies will have a compounding effect on your business. I'm not talking about incremental growth, but that 'overnight' growth you often hear about. These strategies will allow you to unlock rapid growth without it feeling hard or painful.

Most of the strategies I'm going to talk about will help you acquire new customers, but not only new customers, better customers. In some cases that might mean incrementally, so every customer you acquire is better than the last, or it could mean acquiring a massive wedge of customers in one fell swoop.

In many cases, these will be the missing link that's been holding your business back from accelerated growth. But remember that growth isn't linear. There is no flat rate of growth over time; it's lumpy. Some grow significantly and plateau, others may even recede a little. Like children, companies have growth spurts. When I look back at my career, every time one of my companies has had a growth spurt it's because of one of the strategies that I'm about to tell you about.

Before we jump into Chapter 7 though, I'd like to tell you a story that highlights just how important the right knowledge – or in business the right strategies – is to make everything work as it should.

> *The air in the factory is heavy with dust. But there's a silence weighing on everyone on the factory floor. The machinery has stopped. The whole production line has ground to a halt, and it's costing the plant £100,000 an hour because the conveyor belt system isn't working. While some of the workers are taking the chance to enjoy an extended coffee break, the plant manager is tearing his hair out. 'Get hold of an engineer,' he barks at his secretary.*
>
> *When the engineer arrives, he takes a long slow look around the machines, all standing idle, the workers trying to look busy even though they have nothing to do. He sighs and begins a slow and considered walk around the factory floor. He can feel the plant manager's eyes burning into his back, willing him to fix it faster. Slowly and deliberately he makes his way towards an unremarkable cabinet mounted on the wall. He reaches up and opens it, takes a look, inclines his head and then turns to his toolbox. He removes a screwdriver and places it deliberately into one screw, turning it just half an inch. Within seconds the machinery hums into life, sound is restored to the factory, and the familiar clicks, bangs and whoosh of the machinery working are heard again. He*

turns to see the plant manager staring at him, his face a mixture of delight and disbelief. 'That's amazing,' he says, taking the engineer's hand and shaking it. 'Please send me an invoice.' The engineer leaves, the workers return to their stations and the manager heads to his office feeling much relieved.

The next day an invoice from the engineer arrives. The plant manager opens it and stares aghast at the page. The invoice is for £10,000. 'Look at this!' he shouts at his secretary. 'This is just ridiculous; it barely took him any time. I want to know how he thinks he can get away with charging this, go back to him and ask him for a breakdown of his charges.' She dutifully contacts the engineer who sends a second invoice, this time with a breakdown of his charges. It says: 'Turning of screw: £1. Knowing which screw to turn: £9,999.' The plant manager can't argue with that.

That might be an old example, and maybe one you've heard before, but it perfectly illustrates the point that knowing which screw to turn, or in our case which strategies to use when, can change everything. Think of these strategies as that missing piece of knowledge, the final part of your puzzle.

To give you a real example of how the right strategies really can change everything, I'll tell you about one of my clients who took his business from £30,000 a month revenue to £250,000 a month, in a 12 to 18 month period. What you also need to know is that it took him seven years to grow his revenue from £0 to £20,000.

He laid his foundations, and this is vital because you can't have rapid growth without something going spectacularly wrong if you don't have those foundations in place. But after he'd laid those strong foundations, all it took was one key, one strategy, to set his business on a path of very rapid growth.

CHAPTER 7

REACHING IDEAL CLIENTS

I've already mentioned the importance of finding your ideal clients when talking about ramping conversion rates. But in this chapter, I want to dig into who your ideal client is. To do that, I want you to think about the 80/20 principle. I'm sure you've heard of it, but here's a quick refresher. This principle is that 20% of your clients bring in 80% of your revenue.

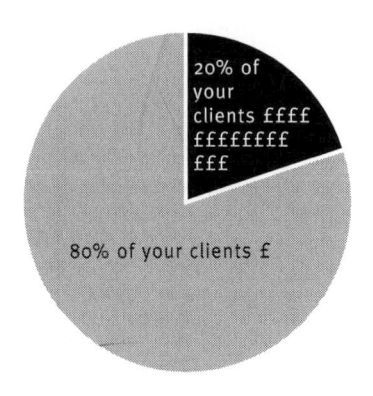

20% of your clients ££££ ££££££££ £££

80% of your clients £

But it goes further than that. The top 20% of that 20% will produce 80% of the revenue brought in by this group of clients.

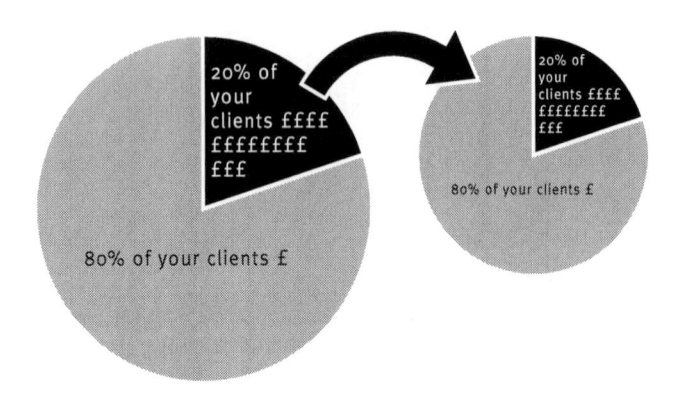

To put that another way, the top 4% of your client base is often responsible for 64% of your revenue. And typically that revenue is more profitable than what you receive from your lower spending clients.

I can show you that this is true because I've done this analysis on my business. Last year, one of my companies had revenue of £2.49 million. It had about 1,300 clients, but the top 20% of them were responsible for £2.2 million of that revenue. However, the top 5% (65 clients) brought in 62% of that revenue, around £1.5 million. What's even more interesting is that my top 13 clients, so 1% of my 1,300 clients, spent more money than the bottom 1,287 combined. In other words, my top 1% was worth more than a thousand times, on average, the ones at the bottom.

You have to look at your broad client demographic, because I'm sure that the majority, if not all, of your clients fall into that broad category. The next step, and the key to finding those ideal clients, is to narrow it down. If you look closely, you'll find demographic and psychographic differences between the clients in your top 4% and the rest. When you know what those differences are you can become more targeted, because why would you try to appeal to just anyone, when you could appeal directly to them and potential clients like them?

NOT ALL CLIENTS ARE EQUAL

Don't misunderstand me; I'm all in favour of equality. But when it comes to business, you can't treat all your clients as though they're the same because they're not. Why would you treat somebody who's going to spend £100,000 with you the same as someone who's going to spend £100? It would be stupid to allocate the same amount of resources you'd put into acquiring a £100,000 client to also wine and dine the £100 person, to convince them to spend money with you. But this is what most people do.

This chapter is about identifying what's different about those ideal clients, and how you can find them. You probably already have the answer in your data.

BUILDING A PICTURE OF YOUR IDEAL CLIENT

Start by looking at your customer data. If you've been in business for any length of time and have had some success, you'll have a lot of useful data. What you need to avoid is looking at that data with any preconceptions. Throw out the idea you have in your head about who your ideal client is. It's very easy to make assumptions about who your ideal clients are, and to then look for evidence that supports that point of view. It's confirmation bias, and it's what most people will do.

But remember, I'm teaching you strategies that most people overlook, and taking a fresh look at your data with no preconceptions of what you might find will bring you results. Your assumptions may be flawed, and the data will show you how you need to change your view of your ideal client. If you can go into this exercise with an open mind, you may spot an unobvious trend.

I'll give you an example from my Mastermind business to help you understand how you can start to build an avatar of your ideal client.

I'd like you to meet Paul. Paul has had moderate success with his business. He's been running his company for at least five years and has a solid revenue stream. His business has no more than two shareholders. He's also focused on his own development and has spent at least £10,000 on this in the past couple of years. Paul is a family man with two young children. He looks after himself and has an interest in improving his health and fitness.

You might look at that profile and see how some of the information helps me, but not understand how it all fits into pinning down those ideal clients. Let me explain.

He's been running a business for at least five years – This is important because they're ready to commit to sustainable changes. They're old enough and have been in business long enough that they're not going to get distracted by the allure of 'I can make millions overnight on Facebook'. They can differentiate the bullshit from the genuinely good value proposition that's going to help their company grow.

His business has no more than two shareholders – My Mastermind programmes are an investment that will benefit a business, but it's a significant spend in the tens of thousands of pounds. That means the shareholders will need to sign off on it. The more shareholders a business has, the harder it is to get a unanimous decision to sign off on that level of investment, and therefore the harder I'll have to work to onboard that client.

He's focused on his own development – This one is crucial in terms of converting people to clients. I want people who already place a high value on investing in their personal and professional development. Then my only job is to show them why investing with me and Mastermind will be superior to investing elsewhere. I'm not having to spend time and energy convincing them that investing in their development is a good idea full stop.

He's got young kids – I honestly don't know why this makes these clients better spenders, but it does. It could be because they're committed to their business in the long term because they don't have one eye on the exit in a couple of years, or it might be that they're trying to build a sustainable enterprise.

He's keen to improve his health and fitness – Not all of my ideal clients fall into this category, but the majority do. That means I use a lot more health and fitness metaphors in my marketing because my ideal clients can relate to them.

When I break it down, it seems obvious, but at one point I was just looking at all these unrecognised threads. Once I started pulling the threads out and putting them together though, it suddenly became obvious who my ideal clients were, and therefore where I could find more of them.

FINDING MORE OF YOUR IDEAL CLIENTS

If you're just realising that the demographic you're targeting is too large, take the time to delve into your data and whittle it down. Being specific is the key to finding more ideal clients.

Think about where you'd look if I asked you to find me clients who fall into this category:

> *I'm looking for anyone who owns a business who might be interested in training. They're between 20 and 60 years old and have a company that's already trading in any industry.*

Now imagine where you'd look if I asked you to find me clients who fall into this category:

> *I'm looking for men aged 35-40, who are married with young children. They've got a company that's at least five years old, and they've spent more than £10,000 on their own personal and professional development in the last couple of years. They've probably also got a bias towards sport or exercise and keeping in shape.*

You can see a clear difference between those two profiles.

CLARITY IS KEY

Having clarity about who your ideal clients are is essential if you're going to find more of them, and not only that, but find more of them in the most efficient way. You can become much more targeted in where you look for clients, and how you market to them. When you define your ideal client to that level, you may also realise you already know some people who fit that demographic.

When it's easier to identify them, it's also easier to convert them. That's because it's a lot easier to go to somebody who fits your demographic with a pitch that's 80% there, than to take that same pitch and try to adapt it to vastly different people. Someone in their 20s who's only been in business a year is going to need a very different pitch to a 65-year-old lady who's been running her business for 45 years and is thinking about retirement.

With clarity also comes a degree of certainty, and that means you can afford to spend more on your marketing, because you know the people you'll be bringing in as clients are going to spend more.

It's a mistake to cap your marketing budget, because that budget should directly correlate to the number of customers you acquire and the value of those customers.

If you're spending £100 to get someone to come to a workshop that they pay £500 for you, you might be making £300, which is an acceptable margin. But if you're trying to get someone to sign up for a coaching programme that's costing £15,000, it's absolutely worth spending more to get them. You don't just want to spend £100; maybe you can justify spending £1,000 in that case because they will bring so much more value to your business.

I know I'd far rather spend £1,000 knowing I'll get £14,000 instead of spending £100 to make maybe £300-£400. Having this clarity and certainty can set you apart from your competitors too. If they'll baulk at spending £100 to acquire a customer, but you're happy to spend £1,000, you can get much more creative with your marketing and offer better incentives. You'll outspend your competitors because you're confident it will work and you know that the customers you attract will spend far more than £1,000 with you.

It's also important to understand that while the top 20% of your clients are where the majority of the value is, the bottom 80% are the cause of most of the stress. More often than not, it's the people who've paid a discounted price, or who've come in on the cheapest deal who cause the most problems. And are the most likely to complain that they're not getting their money's worth.

Despite that being a very typical experience, many business owners will panic about needing more clients, and continue to do things like run offers and discounts to appeal to that bottom 80%. But why?

The antidote to this problem is to clarify who your ideal buyer is and proactively adjust your marketing to speak directly to them. Remember that what attracts your "easy to work with", big spenders is going to be different from what attracts the low-spending clients who cause a lot of stress.

Las Vegas is an excellent example. The big casinos there have slot machines, and they have high roller rooms. Those casinos will market very differently to the person with $100 to spend on the slot machines compared to the person with $100,000 to spend playing Blackjack.

For the $100 spenders you might offer some free food, or free plays to get them through the door. You're going for a high volume, but you know there will be aggravation rolling around that. You're not going to want to spend more than $10-$20 dollars to get them through the door.

For the $100,000 spenders, you pitch the luxury experience. Everything is super deluxe, no expense spared. It's exclusive. You'll happily spend $10,000 or even $20,000 to get them at your table, and having that level of funding at your disposal to attract them makes it much easier because it gives you more options to encourage them to come to your casino. And then stay.

BIRDS OF A FEATHER FLOCK TOGETHER

The more ideal clients you attract, the more you will find. That's because birds of a feather flock together. This leads to what I'm going to talk about in Chapter 8, which is referrals.

If you're a certain type of person, like Paul who I introduced you to earlier in this chapter, you probably know other people like you. If you have a really positive experience of a service or product, you'll share that with other people like you. All of a sudden, your clients can be passing you more clients, who also fall into the demographic of your ideal customer.

When someone is referred, they're much easier to convert. For a start, your clients aren't going to send you people who can't afford your services. They have a trusted relationship with the person they're referring, as well as with you and your business, so that new client already trusts you. Even if the beginning of their experience with you isn't amazing, they're likely to give it a bit more time, because they trust the person who referred them.

But what we're going to look at in the next chapter isn't just about getting referrals from your existing clients. It's about getting referrals from your ideal clients who will bring you more ideal clients. We're looking for more of your big spenders, your top 4%, who will typically convert more quickly and easily and who will typically spend more money with your business.

CHAPTER 8

REFERRAL SYSTEMS

In this chapter, I'm going to introduce you to the concept of referral systems. You might think that you know what referrals are. I'm not just talking about word of mouth; I'm talking about systems that will actively increase your referral rates.

The mistake most people make is that they don't place enough value on referrals. They know they get business through word of mouth, but they treat those leads like any others. That's where they go wrong. In a nutshell, people who come to you via referrals typically convert at a higher rate, convert more quickly, have a higher transaction size, are more likely to stay with the business long term, more likely to give a testimonial, less likely to ask for a refund, and are more likely to give further referrals.

Now you can begin to see why it's so important to treat referrals differently to your other lead sources, and to place greater emphasis on them. If you want to be even more simplistic about it, you could say that referrals are better quality customers because they spend the most and cost the least.

Imagine you're in a room and there are diamonds, gold coins, silver coins and copper coins littered on the floor. Which ones are you going to pick up first? The diamonds, of course, followed by the gold and so on. You might not even bother with the copper ones if you get enough of the diamonds. The point is, referrals are your diamond-standard customers. Think back to Chapter 7 and how great it would be if more of your customers were like your ideal clients. That's what you can get by making proper use of referrals and introducing referral systems.

The reason I know that referrals are the most valuable clients is because of the way we think as people. When you're marketing to people who don't know you, there's a lack of trust. That lack of trust can turn into friction, which means it takes longer and costs more to convince those people who don't trust you to buy from you. If you're selling to someone who's been introduced to you by a person they trust, that friction vanishes. The trust is already there, and that makes it much easier and quicker to close a sale.

That's why referrals are so valuable. The majority of businesses that have been around for any length of time will get business via word of mouth. What most of them fail to do, however, is be systematic about it so that they get the maximum quality and quantity of referrals they can. They don't have a process to drive referrals, they don't measure them, and that means they don't maximise them or improve their process to make it more efficient over time.

THE COMPOUND EFFECT

Many business owners will probably be thinking that's all well and good, but I'm not going to scale my company purely with referrals. Please don't overlook the fact that referrals compound. Imagine that you only have one customer, but that one person brings you two more; and for every customer you get, they also bring you two more. Your business would grow at a geometric rate.

There's a wonderful legend that explains why you shouldn't overlook the importance of compound growth.

One day a peasant saved the life of the King. In his gratitude, the King told the peasant he could have anything he wanted. All the peasant asked was that one grain of rice be placed on a square of a chessboard, and each day double the number of grains of rice would be placed on the next square until the board was full. The King was astounded that this was all the peasant wanted, and readily agreed. There are 64 squares on a chessboard. By day eight, the peasant had 128 grains of rice, by day 16 it had reached 32,868. By day 24 it was up to eight million. By the 64th day, the peasant was owed 18 quintillion grains of rice. Because that sum couldn't be paid, he owned the empire.

Let's bring that back to your business. If you could make one happy customer turn into two additional customers, your business would grow at a compounded rate.

The other thing worth mentioning is that referees are also more likely to buy from you again. So not only do they bring you more customers, but they also spend more themselves.

START WITH YOUR IDEAL CLIENTS

Look at your ideal clients. Where did they come from? I'm willing to bet that the majority came to you via a referral. To a certain degree, that would quantify these clients as more valuable. This is true in virtually every business where I've ever analysed their referrals.

It's not about focusing on referrals to the exclusion of all other forms of lead generation, but about prioritising the lead generation techniques that are going to bring you the best returns. If we say that each referral customer is worth ten times as much as a customer who's come to you from online advertising, then surely that makes it worthwhile to direct some of that advertising spend towards processes, incentives and systems to stimulate word of mouth?

You might be wondering why, if this is true, more people don't do it. There are three main reasons. Firstly, they don't believe it's scalable for the number of clients that they've got. I can tell you now that this isn't true. Secondly, because they're still looking for that one magical thing that will rapidly grow their business. There isn't one. There are lots of ideas, ways, times, places and methods to drive referrals. I'll share some of them with you. But there is not one, single thing that will do it alone. You have to work out which ways will work for your business and how best to implement them. It's complex, and many business owners will shy away from anything that's not easy. If you take the time to introduce a system to stimulate your referrals, you'll have a huge competitive advantage. And thirdly, the reason I gave you at the start of this chapter, which is that the majority of business owners undervalue referrals.

THE FOUR ELEMENTS OF A REFERRAL SYSTEM

There are four elements you need to consider when you're creating a referral system:

- When - when is the optimum time to ask for a referral?
- Who - who can be your best referees?
- Why - what's going to make them want to refer people to you?
- How - how are you going to ask for that referral?

You need to take these four elements and use them to create a checklist to help you determine *who* your best referees will be, *when* you should ask them for a referral and *how* you're going to do it, and *what incentive* they'll have to be an advocate for your business.

When

There is no right or wrong answer to this. There are a number of factors that will influence when you ask for that referral, and they will vary, depending on who you're asking.

Do you ask for the referral up front? Could you offer someone a discount on your product or services if they introduce two people to you who subsequently buy from you? You could even consider making it a condition of the sale. Do you ask someone when they're part-way through the process? If they've signed up for a coaching programme, for example, do you ask them when they've completed half of their sessions and are starting to see the benefits? Or do you wait until the end when they've realised all the benefits?

It's important to understand that asking for referrals at different times will yield different results. You might think that you should ask at all those points, but you need to be careful because what's appropriate will vary from business to business. Always frame these questions in the context of your company.

Who

You might think this one is easy to answer; you're going to ask your customers. But which customers? This ties in with the timing to a certain degree. Do you ask the customers who've just come to one of your workshops, or do you ask the ones who've signed up for the full coaching programme? Or do you contact former customers you've lost touch with? Don't stop with your customers. Can you ask leads who haven't yet made a purchase? Because chances are they will be talking about their decision with different people, so could they introduce more customers to you? What about your suppliers? Could you even ask your competitors?

You might think that asking your competitors for referrals is crazy, but it depends on your business. I've seen it done and work. The logic behind it can be one of two things; either they've bought from me so they might also buy from you, or if they're going to buy from a competitor instead of me, I may as well make some money from it. You could reciprocate and share each other's databases. Maybe my unconverted leads might prefer my competitor and vice versa. I'm not saying all of these will work in your business, but the aim is to stimulate ideas and get you thinking about all the places you might find referrals.

Why

You need to think about why someone would give a referral to you. You could pitch it as a moral obligation. For example, you've recently sold a house, and you went through three rubbish estate agents before you found a good one. It caused you a lot of stress and ultimately meant the process took longer. As the good estate agent, you can ask them if they have any friends who are also selling their house. Could they put them in touch, because they don't want them to go through the same shit experience they had while trying to find a good estate agent?

You can offer a financial incentive for referees. Maybe you give them a discount on a workshop if they bring along two friends, or you could offer a commission. Be careful when it comes to commissions though. A lot of people will think that they need an affiliate referral programme where they offer, say, 10% commission, but this doesn't work in a lot of businesses. For instance, if you have a small margin, you're going to eat into it too much. There's also reputational risk if you agree to act as a referrer for another business without knowing that their products or services are of the highest quality.

Another concept to consider is running a competition where you reward your top referrer. A few years ago I ran a competition among my affiliate marketers for an event I was holding. The affiliate who sold the most tickets to that event won the use of my Ferrari for a week. It worked really well. In rough figures, the affiliate who won drove around £50,000 in additional sales to me, indirectly from initial sales and back-end sales. That doesn't even take into account all the other people who entered the competition and also drove sales to my business. The prize cost me nothing, except that I couldn't drive my own car for a week. But even if I'd had to rent that Ferrari for a week, which would have cost £5,000 for argument's sake, I still would have come out ahead.

You can also offer a special bonus, rather than an obvious financial incentive. Let's use the example of a workshop. I could offer my coaching clients a bonus coaching session after one of my morning workshops that introduces my coaching programme on the condition that they get two people to book onto that morning workshop.

How

Consider how you're going to ask for your referrals and remember that the method you use will change depending on when and who you're asking.

Do you ask face-to-face, which is very low leverage but will probably get the highest conversion? Do you do it on the phone when you call to follow up after a workshop? Do you invite them to share something digitally, whether that's a link on your website or forwarding an email? What about through a podcast? Or a webinar? Or via text message? Or through a Facebook group? There are a lot of options. What you have to consider is that it can be much more personal and lower leverage, which will lead to a higher conversion rate, or it can be entirely automated, systematic and easy for you, but that this will have a lower return.

I saw a great example of the latter recently. Someone shared an article from the Financial Times with me. There's a message built into it asking people who share the article to do so using the sharing tools found on the top right of the page because to copy and paste the content is in breach of the Financial Times' Ts and Cs and copyright policy. So this article has built-in ways for the Financial Times to get referrals. And I was consuming their content, and thinking about whether there was anyone I knew who'd also find it interesting, which is precisely how it came to me.

Their content isn't free; you have to subscribe to access it. But if someone you know and trust sends you an article and says, "Hey, you might find this useful", you're much more likely to pay for a subscription, or at the very least sign up for a trial because they value the content, and therefore you attach a higher value to it.

There are a lot of ways in which you can ask for referrals, but the key is not to be overbearing. You need to choose the right method for the right people and present it at the right time.

MAKE SURE YOU'RE REFERABLE

None of this is any good, however, if you don't have a referable business. It doesn't matter when you ask, how you ask, what incentives you give or who you ask, if you don't have happy customers who've had a great experience with you. This ties back into the earlier chapters of the book but specifically Chapter 3 and retention. You need to make it easy for them to want to tell their friends about how great you and your product or service are.

You have to remove friction from every step of the process. So firstly you need to make your customers believe that you're worth referring. You do that by giving them a great experience. You have to make it easy for them to refer people to you. That might mean having those shareable links embedded in your online content, or making sure you give such a great service that no one is worried about referring people to you.

The same thing goes if I'm asking a competitor or supplier to refer for me. I have to give them something simple, like content they can copy and paste into an email to send out to their database for example. You also have to make sure that what you're asking them to refer is appropriate.

For example, if I want a referral for my Mastermind coaching programme, which costs £15,000, I'm not going to ask someone to send out an email to their contacts. I'm going to want to have face-to-face interactions. Also, you won't want to ask all of your contacts to make such a big financial commitment. There's the worry that it won't work for them, and then they've spent £15,000 and will partially blame you that they wasted that money. It causes friction. But if I'm running a workshop that costs just £500 to attend, it's much easier for someone to feel comfortable sharing that with their contacts. It's lower risk because they're only spending £500 and even if they only think it's 'ok', it's not going to do too much damage in the grand scheme of things.

But more important than anything is being referable so that anyone who's referring for you knows that you'll deliver. That's how to make it easy for people to give you endorsements.

CREATING THE RIGHT REFERRAL SYSTEM FOR YOUR BUSINESS

There is no one-size-fits-all approach to creating referral systems. I can't give you a magic formula that will work every time, no matter your company or the industry you operate in. Those kinds of things don't exist. What I'm offering you are the tools to create a referral system that's right for your business.

I've just given you a checklist of four things to consider. Start there. Make a list of all the things you could do for your company, who you could approach and so on. Once you have that, rank those ideas in terms of which logically make the most sense and are the easiest to implement.

Consider which options will generate the highest quality referrals, which ones are least likely to piss your clients off, and which ones are the easiest to implement in your company.

Remember that you're going to be asking different people – or sometimes the same people at different stages of their journey with you – to refer people in different ways. So, I might ask my Mastermind members to refer people to specific workshops. I might be asking past workshop attendees to encourage others to come along to workshops. But I might just be sharing my latest podcast with my whole database and asking them to share that podcast with their friends. I'll approach each of those scenarios differently. For the first one, I might have that conversation in a face-to-face meeting. The second one might be part of a follow-up phone call after a workshop. And the third one will be a link in an email.

The next stage, once you have your ranked list of ideas, is crucial. You test them. You absolutely have to test your ideas on a small scale before you roll them out to your whole client base. And you need to tweak them as you go.

Let's use my Mastermind coaching business as an example again. If I announced to all my existing Mastermind clients that they could get their next year's membership free by getting a friend to join I might end up with lots of new clients, but I'll also annihilate my profits. I might now have two members, but I'm only getting £10,000 for both of them, instead of £10,000 each. More than that, my existing member would have paid £10,000 for their second year of membership, and I wouldn't have had any costs associated with it. I wouldn't have had to pay commission or spend money getting them onboard. So I've lost even more. And what do I do if someone comes to me and says they've already brought me three new clients this year? Do I give them three years of free membership? All of a sudden my costs have gone up, but my revenue has gone down. Sometimes you can make a bold move like that and it can pay off, but other times it can land you in deep shit. So you always have to ask yourself, how can you safely test your ideas?

Another way to approach this example would be for me to informally approach just one or two of my Mastermind members who are up for renewal and say, 'Hey Paul, you're up for renewal, do you think you might know anyone else who'd like to join Mastermind? I'll offer you a special deal for your second year if you can bring me a new member. I've not tried this before, but could you help me test it?' And Paul goes, 'Hell yes. In fact Dan, if you offer me 50% commission, then I'll bring you two new people.' And he comes back with two new clients, and I think 'holy crap', so I start to roll it out with a couple more of my members.

As I try it with new people, maybe I tweak it slightly. So for every new member a client brings to the programme, they get £5,000 off their next year's membership. So if Paul brings me two new people, who are each paying £10,000, that means he gets a year free.

But you always have to think about how you can tweak things to make sure you're still making more profit from your referrals. How you do that will vary depending on your business. If you've got a low-margin but an expensive product you're going to tread a lot more carefully. Maybe you limit the number of referrals someone can bring, only run an offer for a limited time, or cap the number of times someone can win a competition.

How you test will come down to the likely damage it could cause and the likely upside of the ease of execution. So if you minimise the number of people who can take advantage of an offer, or limit the time it runs for, you've probably minimised a lot of the risk just by considering that.

WHEN REFERRALS GO RIGHT...

An early business of mine specialised in providing marketing consulting to professionals in neuro-linguistic programming (NLP). I had around 50 clients, and the business was making low six-figure revenues. I was great at converting people, but I struggled with lead generation. I didn't know how to tap into the big market of NLP-qualified professionals. I kept thinking about how I could reach out to people with these qualifications and decided I needed to target NLP organisations. I made a list of all the NLP organisations in the UK, and one jumped out at me. It had the largest database of NLP professionals in the country at the time, 80,000 people. It was perfect.

I looked at the company much more closely and realised that although they had lead generation figured out, their conversion rates weren't great and most people didn't spend a lot of money with them. I scrolled through landing page after landing page, and they were just terrible. I knew it wouldn't take much to improve them. My strength was in my marketing and conversions, so now I had a way to get in front of Jamie, the CEO, and pitch my idea.

But I didn't know Jamie, and there was no reason for him to trust me. I had to be careful how I went about this. I arranged a meeting with him. I made sure I looked the part and although I was nervous I was quietly confident. When I walked into the meeting I smiled, went through the introductions and then launched into my pitch. I could feel Jamie warming up to my idea as I talked.

"I'd really like to go into a joint venture with you," I said, "But I know that you don't know me yet or trust me." He just watched me as I continued, "So, I'm going to propose that I do something for you and your business, with no obligation on you, to prove that I'm serious and to show you how well our companies could work together."

"OK," Jamie said, hesitantly. I could tell he was intrigued, but I knew I hadn't convinced him yet. "What are you spending on your marketing each month?" I asked. "£10,000," Jamie replied. "And how many leads do you get a month for that?" I asked. "Roughly 1,000," he said. I took a deep breath; it was time for my big pitch. "What if I told you I could double the capture rate for your landing page, without you spending a penny more?"

Jamie raised his eyebrows. "So you're saying you can get me 2,000 leads a month for the same £10k spend?". "Yes," I said. "And I'll do it entirely at my own risk, on my own time and at my own cost. I'll even split test my landing page next to yours to prove that mine converts better. If I'm right, that will make you a lot of money."

"Yes, it will," Jamie responded. I could see that I had him, now it was time to deliver the final part of the deal. "If I do this for your business, would you be happy to discuss a joint venture with me, where you give my business referrals?" "Yes, absolutely," Jamie agreed. We shook hands, finished the meeting and I left.

I was buzzing about the opportunity and couldn't wait to get started. I used all my knowledge from my marketing experience to improve their landing page. We agreed that we'd test it alongside the existing landing page for a week. All week I watched as the results rolled in and I couldn't believe my eyes. At the end of the seven days, I was ready to go back to Jamie, and I was beaming. There was a 102.6% improvement in the capture rate with my landing page.

I walked into my meeting with Jamie with my head held high. I knew he'd seen the results of my work. I smiled, "So, can we discuss that joint venture now?" Jamie looked at me and just said three words, "No discussion necessary." My heart sank like a stone. Surely he couldn't be telling me that after all I'd done he wouldn't even consider working with me? He must have seen the look on my face because he smiled. "After the results you provided I'll do whatever you'd like. If you want me to send an email then get it over to me, and I'll make sure it's sent out to our database," he said. I felt like I'd been holding my breath. I exhaled and my despair quickly turned to elation again. I'd done it.

I created a whole new product just for this email. I wanted something that would work as a low price entry product because that was what was missing from what I already offered. What I was after were qualified leads. I put together a CD set, specifically about marketing for

NLP professionals. In the email, I offered this product just for the cost of postage and packaging, which might be commonplace now but it was a rarity back then. Jamie sent my email offering this product, and within 48 hours I had 800 new customers for my business. I knew I wasn't going to get rich from sending a CD set out and charging under £3 for it, but that didn't matter. Now I had what I'd needed all along: NLP professionals who were interested in improving the marketing of their businesses.

From those 800, I got around 100 to attend workshops over the coming weeks. I averaged around £1,000 per sale, per person that came to each of my workshops. Within about six weeks of that referral system starting, I'd made around £120,000.

But that's not the end of this story. Although it was a highly leveraged referrals system, I made my business highly referable because I was offering a great product at a very low cost. That, in turn, allowed me to build relationships with those contacts and get more of them to come to my workshops and so on. It went even further than that though. I eventually worked out how to buy Jamie's company. That meant I had the benefit of a fully functioning, profitable company, and I now had 80,000 new customers whom I could refer to my original business that offered complementary products and services.

All of this leads nicely onto our final chapter about roll ups. Until this point, I've been talking about getting solid foundations in place and once you have those, it's simply a matter of attracting more of the right calibre of customers. Referral systems are a highly leveraged way of doing just that, but there's one way which is even faster...

CHAPTER 9

ROLLING UP

This chapter is about one of the most potent strategies to accelerate your business growth: roll-up. A roll-up is a term used to describe pulling together two or more companies in a similar market and putting them into one basket. By doing so, you drive up profit across both businesses due to cross-selling opportunities, cost savings and other synergies.

If you look at all successful business people, once their company has reached a certain size, they take a different approach to growth. They grow their businesses through mergers and acquisitions (M&A). In the UK, domestic M&A activity was worth £26.5 billion in 2018[3]. It's a massive industry, and that makes sense because it's the highest leverage activity. You can acquire a customer, but acquiring

---

[3] https://www.ons.gov.uk/businessindustryandtrade/changestobusiness/mergersandacquisitions

a business doesn't only mean you acquire their customers, you also acquire their systems, and that allows you to acquire new customers on an ongoing basis.

WHY USE ROLLING UP TO GROW YOUR BUSINESS?

Let's have a look at a simple example to show you how roll-ups can be so effective when they're done right.

We have Company A and Company B. Both operate in the same industry. They're each making £500,000 in revenue and generating £100,000 profit. If you put them together, two main things will happen.

Synergies

Firstly, the customers from Company A will buy products from Company B, without Company B having to spend any more on marketing. It's cheap, or even free, to market to Company A's customers now. With no customer acquisition cost, revenue increases, but more importantly, profitable revenue increases because you have lower marketing costs. This works both ways.

Efficiencies

Secondly, there are a host of cost savings and efficiencies that can be made across the two businesses. Now that they're one, you only need one insurance policy, for example. You may not need to run two offices. You may only need one bookkeeper, etc.

Now you have to look back at the figures. It's not as simple as putting Company A's revenue and profits with Company B's revenue and profits. With rolling up, 1+1 doesn't equal two. It equals more than two.

Company A had revenue of £500,000 and profit of £100,000.
Company B had revenue of £500,000 and profit of £100,000.
Together though they have revenue of £1.2 million and profit of £400,000, because of those synergies, efficiencies and cost savings I just talked about.

M&A can also have an impact on a company's overall valuation. When companies are bought and sold the price is dictated not so much by how much money they make now, but by how much money they are predicted to make in the future. For the new owner, it will be about how reliable, predictable and sustainable it is. Or another way to look at it is how low risk it is to make that additional money.

There are many ways of valuing companies, but to keep things simple I'm going to use the price-to-earnings, or P/E, ratio. This is essentially the price of a share shown as a multiple of the earnings.

Let's say that Company XYZ has a P/E ratio of 14. That means that at this moment in time, Company XYZ is worth 14 times its annual profit. That's a very high P/E ratio. Most small businesses will have one that's much lower. In 2018, the average in the UK was 2.96 amongst small businesses. But the P/E ratio isn't just determined by the size of the business; it's also determined by the industry it operates in.

For example, a mobile phone company will have a higher P/E ratio, and therefore a higher valuation than a retail store of a similar size. Why? Because the mobile phone company's income is based on a higher amount of contracted revenue, whereas the retail store has a much higher risk level and its profits aren't as certain.

How does this relate to you and your business? If you look back at our first example of merging Company A and Company B, you're probably going to see increased revenue and increased profit. However, even if that didn't happen, the new company you've created will typically have a higher P/E ratio than Company A or Company B had on their own. That's because in merging the two, you've now got a wider range of customers, more products and services, and fewer single points of failure. Maybe it can operate in different markets. But ultimately it's become less dependent on you. Its profits are more stable, and there are fewer things that could see it all come crashing down.

Company A, with its £500,000 revenue and £100,000 profit has a P/E ratio of 3. That means you bought it for £300,000 and merged it with Company B.

Company B, with its £500,000 revenue and £100,000 profit also has a P/E ratio of 3.

But now that they're together, the value isn't £600,000. It will be higher than that because there's additional revenue growth, profit savings, and the business has become more stable. In our original example, we said that merging Company A and Company B led to profits increasing to £400,000. Because the new business is more stable, let's assume the P/E ratio has increased to 4.

Your original company was worth £300,000. By rolling up with another similar-sized business, you now have a company that's worth £1.6 million (£400,000 x 4).

That's the power of rolling up. It's also why most larger companies don't grow from scratch, they grow from acquisitions because it's a lot quicker, in some respects it can be a lot safer, and it's cheaper.

FINDING ACCRETIVE

Accretive is an investment term that means a company you buy pays for itself; so in real terms, it costs me nothing to buy your business. I may have to move money around to pay you for the acquisition of your business, but when the dust settles, it won't have cost me a penny. That might be because due to my experience, your business rolled up into my company, can quickly generate a lot more revenue. Or it might be because I've bought your business for £8 million, for example, but it holds £28 million in stock, so even if I sold all that stock at cost price, I'd still make £20 million. And that's the worst case scenario for that acquisition. What I'd be hoping to do is turn that business around and be in a position to sell it for far more than £8 million in the future.

These kinds of opportunities are all around. You want to look for companies that are struggling on their own, but that you know in your hands can immediately become profitable. You often get far more than a profitable business out of it too. You'll get a lot of new customers, systems, additional products to sell and maybe even more great employees. That's what happened when I bought a company some years ago.

> *I noticed the business before I decided to buy it. I was keeping an eye on it as they operated in the same sector as one of my companies and it always pays to check in on the competition. After a number of months, I realised they weren't doing so well, and I knew it was time to make my move. When I bought this business, it wasn't particularly lucrative, but I knew that merging it with my company would make it stronger.*

But there was another reason I wanted this particular company; because of its Managing Director. I'd been keeping an eye on him too, and I could see that he was doing a good job with the business, but he needed a bit of guidance and oversight from me to do a great job. This played into my hands because I was keen to take a step back from this particular company.

I acquired this competing business and rolled it into my company, and I kept the MD. It didn't take long for the acquisition to pay off; we were making more profit in a short space of time, and I now had someone to keep on top of everything, freeing me up to focus on other projects. In that first year, we grew our profits substantially, and I freed up more and more of my time until I was able to 'fire' myself from that business.

FOUNDATIONS COME FIRST

As you've probably gathered by now, roll-ups are a very powerful strategy, and a higher than average way to accelerate your growth. You might be wondering why I'm only introducing this now, in the final chapter of the book. The reason is simple: without implementing the strategies from the preceding eight chapters, roll-ups are reckless.

It's easy to get carried away with growth strategies in your business, but if you don't have the foundations in place to support a much larger, faster-growing business, you're going to run into trouble. If you've followed the advice I've given in *Defend* and *Develop*, you're now probably running a much more efficient and stronger company than your competitors. That means their company in your hands is worth a lot more to you than it is to them. That's the perfect time to use this strategy to accelerate your growth. But, if you don't have those fundamentals right, rushing to acquire another company is likely to be a recipe for disaster. It all comes back to that compounding effect.

Remember the Bill Gates quote? *"The first rule of any technology used in business is that automation applied to an efficient operation will magnify the efficiency. The second is that automation applied to an inefficient operation will magnify the inefficiency."*

Rolling up has a compounding effect. That can mean a compounding effect in a good way, but it can have a disastrous compounding effect if you don't know what you're doing and are losing money.

HOW TO TELL IF YOU'RE READY FOR ROLLING UP

Obviously, you don't want to try to roll up until you're ready. But how do you know when that is? There are three main things you need to consider before you start looking for other businesses to acquire.

1. **The state of your current company:** Is your current company well run? Is it stable? Is it making a profit? How have you applied some of the principles in this book? This is what you need to get in order first.

2. **Capital:** If your own company is running well, it should be producing a profit, and that means there's some money to invest. Although you can borrow money to buy other companies, you want to be in a reasonably

stable financial position because these things can go wrong and cost a lot of money. You also want to make sure that you personally are in a stable financial position.

3. **Good advisors:** This one is crucial if you're going to roll up a company successfully. I would personally insist that you seek advice from three types of people: accountants, lawyers with M&A experience, and mentors who have bought and sold companies and been through the process you're about to embark on.

Of those three, mentors are the most important and probably the hardest to find. The reason you want a mentor, or multiple mentors, is because they will know the pitfalls. They may even have made some of the mistakes themselves, and they can save you a lot of money and stress by helping you dodge those bullets. It's about risk mitigation. Roll-ups are an incredibly powerful strategy, but they can and do bankrupt people. You need to go into them with your eyes open. Being rich won't protect you if you make fundamental errors.

One of my most profound realisations was that life cares about results, not how you got there. Life doesn't reward you more because you toiled more to achieve a particular result. If you pay a pile of money into a bank, do they give you extra because first you created fire, then you invented the wheel? Of course not. It doesn't matter if a sale took you ten hours or ten weeks to close; the result is the same. So why would you do a roll-up the longer, harder way, if you could expedite it and learn through the experience of others? It's the key to progressing faster with lower risk.

HOW TO FIND A MENTOR

When you're looking for a mentor to help you with rolling up, the most important thing is that they've been there and done it; the more experience they have, the better.

But a very close second is someone who will challenge your way of thinking. Maybe even someone with very strong opinions that are different from your own. You need someone who can give you advice without bias. You need to know that their advice comes from their experiences, and that they aren't tailoring it just to keep you happy. That's why I'd be wary of having a mentor whose sole income comes from advising others, because they might not be as blunt as you need them to be, because they're worried about losing you as a client.

That said, I'm not saying don't pay for advice, because there is massive value in good-quality paid for advice. What you want to avoid at all costs is doing this on the cheap. Don't just try and pick up snippets of information here and there by taking friends of friends out for coffee, because often a little bit of information is the worst thing.

Even if you're not looking for a mentor to advise you on rolling up, it's still worth seeking out people who will challenge your thinking. You'll learn a lot and get a more balanced perspective. You want to find people whose opinion you respect, and you want to ask them to help you understand their point of view. That doesn't mean you have to change your opinion of a particular area, but by listening to someone on the other side of the argument you'll better understand it, and you'll develop a broader range of tools that you can use in your business.

We all have different strengths. Some of us are very numbers focused, whereas others are much more people oriented. Both have valuable skills that are essential in running successful businesses and the more you can develop your weaker side the better.

> *Ten years ago I was struggling to push one of my businesses over the £500,000 mark with its revenue. No matter what I did, I kept getting stuck. I remember looking around at other successful business people. I was intrigued by one in particular, who had a net worth of over $100 million but some of the worst marketing I'd ever seen. Marketing was my strength, and it would have been easy for me to dismiss this guy and move on. But something told me I needed to learn from him. Yes, his marketing was terrible, but he was infinitely more successful than me. Why? What was he doing that I wasn't? I managed to get out of my ego for just long enough to recognise this void.*
>
> *During our first meeting, it didn't take him long to see where my problems lay. They were as clear as day to him. He looked at my documents and gave me one piece of advice: Go away and develop your financial literacy. At this time I was financially illiterate, I didn't understand my figures. He was an accountant, and numbers were his thing. By going to him for advice, I'd taken myself out of my comfort zone. I'd known deep down that he wouldn't be impressed by all the flashy marketing in the world and that was why getting advice from him was so valuable. He challenged my way of thinking. What he told me that day was a game changer. Figures and accounting went from being my greatest area of weakness to probably one of my greatest strengths. Now I'm a numbers man through and through.*

DEAL FLOW

Another important way to prepare for rolling up is to put yourself in an environment where you get exposed to a lot of potential transactions, specifically those relating to rolling up companies. Finding a mentor is the broader principle at work, because you're spending time with one person who has been there and done it. You can benefit from their experience and learn vicariously by looking over their shoulder.

But remember that birds of a feather flock together. That means people who frequently buy and sell companies typically know other people who do the same. If you can start spending more time with them, you'll get exposed to a greater number of transactions.

You might learn new ways to approach things, or hear about risks you hadn't considered. It's all part of the wider theme of this book, which is making yourself a better business owner.

PRACTICAL CONSIDERATIONS WHEN BUYING A COMPANY

Look for synergies

Firstly, when it comes to rolling up, the greatest synergies are going to be found in businesses that are exactly like yours, so start by looking at your competitors. For example, I own a gym, so I could buy out another local gym. I can close that gym, but move all its members onto contracts at my gym. Another way to approach it is to look for a complementary business. So, maybe I look at rolling up with a company that manufactures gym kit, because I can sell some of their products at my gym, as well as having the benefits of the business selling gym kit elsewhere.

You have to look up and down your supply chain to work out what will bring you the greatest benefits. I have a client who has a chain of weight loss clinics, and he rolled up with another chain of weight loss clinics. That made his business much larger. But it had one big risk. As part of the service, they provided meal replacements for all the customers on their weight loss plans, but all those meals came from just one provider.

His next step was to buy that supplier. This had several positive effects. Firstly, it reduced their costs, because instead of paying the retail price for their food, they paid the wholesale price. Secondly, they instantly gained additional profits, because this supplier didn't just provide meals for them, it also provided meals to other weight loss businesses in the country. Thirdly, this made my client much more aware of how businesses in the sector were performing. He can now see how many meals other clinics are buying, and has a reasonably good idea of what their sales revenue is. That's a great example of how rolling up a complementary business can be beneficial.

Avoid brokers

Generally speaking, I'd advise against buying through a business broker. You have to think of business brokers as a little bit like estate agents. When you decide to sell your house, you'll ask three agents to give you a valuation. Most people will then list with the agent who provides them with the highest valuation for their property. It's no different in business.

A business broker will typically get an upfront fee for listing your business, so it's in their interests to list as many companies as possible. Here's an example of what might happen:

You're planning to sell your business. It's doing ok and is worth £300,000. But you've never sold a business before, so you get three brokers to give you valuations. One values it at £500,000, one at £600,000 and one at £800,000. You're probably going to list with the one who values it at £800,000 because you don't realise your business is worth nowhere near that much, and that it almost certainly won't sell.

Then I come in, as someone who has experience of buying and selling businesses. I look at your figures, and I offer you a price that I think is sensible; I offer you £300,000, which is what it's actually worth. But you don't know any better, and you find that massively insulting because it's so far below the valuation the broker has given you.

Now I'm not saying it's impossible to get a good deal on a business through a broker. I am saying it's a lot more difficult, because often the business owner will have unrealistic expectations about what their business is worth.

Often, the best businesses to buy aren't the ones for sale. My advice is to keep a close eye on your competitors when you're ready to think about rolling up. Network with people in your industry, see what they're doing and maybe even approach some of them and tell them that, if they ever thought of selling, you'd be interested. Just plant that seed and walk away.

Emotions are the enemy

It can be easy to get emotionally attached to our businesses, and that works against you when it comes to selling them.

If you allow your emotions to creep in, you'll believe the broker who values your company at £1 million when really it's worth half that. You'll get greedy, and you won't find anyone to buy from you at that price. You might even take your head out of the game because, mentally, you're ready to move on. That can be disastrous, because your company's performance can go downhill and the value of your business can decline. You have to stay emotionally unattached and look at it purely from an investment perspective.

But it's also important not to get carried away when you're buying a business. You have to look at things from an investor's point of view, and not get too excited. If you're emotional about the acquisition, you're going to make stupid choices. You'll think a company is worth more than it is, and that's when you take on too much risk and screw it up.

HOW I KNEW I WAS READY TO ROLL UP

It's 2012, I'm fit, strong and love competing. My latest thing is Iron Man races. They take triathlons to a whole new level, and I can't get enough. I'm on the starting line, shoulder to shoulder with the other guys, all raring to go, ready to jump into that cold water at the sound of the horn. I take a deep breath, dive in, and I'm in a flurry of white water, swimming, breathing, keeping a good pace. I'm out at the other end, running into the transition ready to jump on my bike.

I pull on my cycling shoes, strap on my helmet, grab my bike out of the rack and climb on. My feet click effortlessly into the cleats on the pedals, and now I'm flying. My legs felt a little sluggish from the swim, but they're warming up nicely. I know I'm pacing it well and making good time. I hit a corner a little too hard, all of a sudden my wheel wobbles, I'm losing control, and I'm off the course. In a split second, I'm thrown from the bike. I barely have time to register the tree before everything goes black.

I wake up in hospital to the sound of beeps and the low murmur of nurses. I'm told that I hit the tree so hard I split my helmet and that I've suffered brain damage. The following eight months are a blur of hospital wards and slow steps towards becoming healthy again. I needed neurorehabilitation, and it was a long road to recovery. But it was at this time that I realised I needed to take my business to the next level.

By this point, I'd been running my own companies for nearly ten years. I'd had the best part of a decade of making a good, six-figure income, but I wasn't financially free. I wasn't massively in debt, just a mortgage, and I had some savings, but while I was lying in one of those hospital beds, I realised that if I died or was unable to work again, it wouldn't be too long before my wife had to go back to work. That, to me, was crazy. And that was when I realised I needed to build some wealth.

I started looking around and realised that the wealthiest people in the UK didn't get there by running successful businesses; they got there by selling them. Look at all the dragons on Dragon's Den as an example – every single one has made their millions from selling businesses that they've made successful. I needed to change my approach.

At this point, I had three businesses, but the problem was that all three were dependent on me. If I wanted to sell one and make my family financially secure for life, I needed to make some changes. So, I bought a competitor to one of my three businesses. Remember the story I told you earlier, about finding the business with the MD? That's the one I bought and rolled up with one of my companies. Now I had a business that could run perfectly well without me, that was making a good profit and that I could sell. I want to share the figures with you though, so that you can understand just how much of a difference rolling up can make to a business' value.

I had an offer on the company I wanted to sell, which came in at around £60,000. Basically, the buyer was just interested in my database. That wasn't enough, so I went away and found this competitor to roll up. I bought that company using an accretive deal, which meant I didn't need to find any money up front. I asked the owner how much he wanted for the business and he told me £100,000. That's what I bought it for on paper. We agreed that I'd merge the companies and sell them on. I'd pay him his £100,000 and keep the rest.

The businesses were a natural fit. The company I bought was really strong from an operations perspective, but had a terrible sales and marketing department. My company, on the other hand, was really strong in sales and marketing, but weaker on the operational side. By putting the two together, both businesses became infinitely more efficient.

In less than six months, I'd merged the companies and sold to an American buyer for around £650,000. I paid the original owner of the second company his £100,000 and took the remainder. I went from a company being valued at £60,000 to selling it for £650,000 within six months, just by rolling up.

CONCLUSION

To summarise what I've explained over the last nine chapters, this book has been about how to maximise the value of your company, how to have it make more money, and be less dependent on you. When you started reading, your company might have been at the very beginning of this process. But I'm sure that by now you have a whole variety of ideas for each of the steps in this structure, and that will allow you to build on what you have and move forward.

LET'S BRIEFLY RECAP EACH OF THOSE NINE AND A HALF STEPS

Risk mitigation

This is about looking at what the biggest threats to your company are, how to lessen the risk of those occurring and how to minimise the damage if they do. Do this, and you'll make money with less stress. Drama costs money.

Reducing expense ratios

Every company wastes money, and every single penny that the company spends is an investment in itself. But some of that investment is poorly managed. By reducing those expenses and reallocating those savings towards the most profitable part of the business, you can grow at a much more rapid pace.

Retention of existing clients

There is no point in filling a leaky bucket. How big would your business be if you still had every customer who had ever tried you? Having happy customers is not only more enjoyable, but it's also much more profitable to retain a customer than go and get a new one. And of course, don't forget the half-step the title of this book refers to – reactivation. If you have clients you've let go after you've provided your product/service and haven't resold to or even spoken with in some time, make sure you reactivate the relationship. You'll be amazed at the opportunities a simple phone call can uncover.

Repeat purchases

If you have happy customers, give them more opportunities to spend money with you, again and again and again. How might you do that? What kind of recurring transaction can you create?

Raising AOV (average order value)

Can you have a good, better, best option? How do you get the people in your metaphorical supermarket to spend more money when they're there, by either putting more items in their trolley or more expensive items in their trolley?

Ramping conversion rates

You already have a process, you're spending money for leads, and you're trying to get them to become your customers. It costs typically nothing, or minimal amounts of money, to significantly increase your conversion rates so that more of those leads become paying customers. How do you optimise each step in your sales process and/or add more steps? Remember, 80% of people buy after more than five contact points from a company, but 80% of companies stop marketing after just two contacts with a lead.

Reaching ideal clients

This is the Pareto principle to the second power. 20% of your customers are typically responsible for 80% of your profits. Yet the top 20% of that 20%, i.e. 4% of your overall customer base, gets you 80% of the 80%, i.e. 64% of your profits. If you profile this 4% of customers, you'll often find that they are very different than your average customer. By identifying this, you can market more effectively to them and get more of those ideal customers.

Referral systems

The best customer is somebody that spends the most but costs the least. People that come via referral buy more quickly; buy at a higher rate; spend more money; and stick around longer. They are the ideal clients. But are you actively maximising the number of referrals you get from your already satisfied clients?

Rolling up

Once you've got the foundations in place, the quickest way to multiply your company's growth and valuation will be to buy other either competitive or complementary companies and maximise the synergies by combining those businesses.

When you apply all nine and a half of these steps, not only will your profits increase, but so will the reliability, predictability and sustainability of those profits. In other words, you'll make more money with less stress, which will make your company significantly more valuable if you choose to exit. And also significantly more enjoyable should you choose to keep it. However, the ideas you have to implement those nine and a half steps literally have no value unless they're applied. The key now is to think about how you're going to apply them. In the 15 years I've worked with other businesses, I've learned there is no one-size-fits-all solution.

However, the principle I'd like to leave you with is that if you spend time around smart, ambitious people, great things happen. If you want to raise your tennis game, you play against people who are a little better than you. In much the same way, if you spend time with other business owners who are smart, ambitious and have already done the things that you want to do, your business improves. Do this and watch your company thrive.

Conclusion

If you've enjoyed this book and want to get some more great free resources, head over to danbradbury.com, or subscribe to the Business Growth Show with Dan Bradbury on iTunes, or wherever you get your podcasts, and keep yourself up to date.

Remember, if you want your company to grow, you need to grow.

ABOUT THE AUTHOR

Dan Bradbury is an investor specialising in taking companies that are already producing multiple six figures in revenue and accelerating their growth to over £10 million. In his 20s he built and sold his first business for over £1 million. At 31, Dan turned around a company that was listed on the U.S. stock market for $4.3 million. He has worked with over 8,000 business owners in 69 different countries worldwide.

If you've enjoyed this book and believe others will also find it useful, please help them make the decision to read it by leaving your review on Amazon.co.uk.

Printed in Great Britain
by Amazon